BALWANT GARGI, playwright-director-film maker, was born in a sandy village in Punjab in 1916. He studied at Lahore and received his M.A. in English literature. Writer of 35 one-act plays, 10 full-length dramas and numerous stories and critical articles, his plays have been staged in Moscow, and Seattle and by the major theatre groups in India. He received the Sahitya Akademi Award for *Theatre in India* (1962), the Watumull Special Achievements Award for *Folk Theatre of India* (1967), *Padma Shree* (1972), and the International (Asian) Film Festival Award for his colour documentary *Jatra* (1976.)

He taught and directed classical and folk dramas at the University of Washington, Seattle, and was Founder-Director of the Department of Indian Theatre at Panjab University, Chandigarh (1968 to 1977).

Currently, he is settled in New Delhi as a writer and film maker.

Also by the same author

THE NAKED TRIANGLE

PURPLE MOONLIGHT

Balwant Gargi

UBSPD
UBS Publishers' Distributors Ltd.
New Delhi Bombay Bangalore Madras
Calcutta Patna Kanpur London

UBS Publishers' Distributors Ltd.
5 Ansari Road, New Delhi-110 002
Bombay Bangalore Madras
Calcutta Patna Kanpur London

© Balwant Gargi

First Published   1993
First Reprint   1993

All rights reserved. No part of this publication may be reproduced or transmitted in any form or by any means, electronically or mechanically, including photocopying, recording or any information storage or retrieval system, without prior permission in writing from the publisher or in accordance with the provisions of the Copyright Act 1956 (as amended). Any person who does any unauthorized act in relation to this publication may be liable to criminal prosecution and civil claims for damages.

Cover Sketch : JATIN DAS
Cover Design : MAHENDRA

This title is available both in Hardback and Paperback Editions.

PB   ISBN 81-85674-03-5

Lasertypeset by Alphabets, New Delhi and printed at Rajkamal Electric Press, B-35/9, G.T. Karnal Road Industrial Area, Delhi

to
Rose Mary Brennan

I am grateful to J.S. Butalia for his valuable suggestions, and to my son Manu for going over the book patiently.

–B.G.

"Memories are not history but original creations by the unseen artist. The diverse colours scattered about are not reflections of the outside world but belong to the painter himself, and come passion-tinged from the heart — thereby making the record on the canvas unfit for use as evidence in a court of law... So it is as literary material that I offer my memory pictures. To regard them as an attempt at autobiography would be a mistake."

--Rabindranath Tagore

1

During Partition I moved from Lahore to Delhi through a blood-bath. Hordes of men filled with savage hate attacked innocent people. They hacked off men's genitals, amputated women's breasts, and sported children's heads on their spears as trophies, shouting glory to Mahadeva, to Allah, and to Waheguru. When their frenzy subsided, they marched in the streets singing slogans of communal harmony and human brotherhood.

The mute gods smiled in the heavens as they looked down on their devotees.

Like millions of refugees, I searched for lodging, and found the annexe of a ravaged bungalow. It consisted of two rooms, a courtyard with a champa plant, a kitchen, and a verandah with Arab arches. Before Partition, these rooms had been occupied by two employees of a Muslim nawab who had fled to Pakistan. The bungalow, mortgaged by a Hindu dentist to the nawab, was repossessed by the dentist—a humped, greasy-tongued Uriah Heep–who rented it to me on a high charge. He often boasted of his professional skill, and told me that he had extracted two teeth of Mahatma Gandhi and treated many political leaders.

The house was located in a lively neighbourhood between Curzon Road (now Kasturba Gandhi Marg) and Queensway (now Janpath)—the two radial streets shooting out of the outer circle of Connaught Place, a fashionable shopping centre.

I moved in at once.

That night the sky burst, flooding roads, parks, and houses. Lightning flashed through black clouds like a negress baring her teeth. In the morning, when the sun shone, Delhi was washed of its bloodstains.

A few months later, jobless and bored with Delhi, I left for Bombay. The city had always fascinated me with its tropical settings: tall feathery palms, sooty tea shops, huts, dried fish, the fabled film world and the ocean which circled it like a ripped blue skirt

I stayed with Mulk Raj Anand, novelist and cultural uncle, in his posh apartment at Cuffe Parade. He did not ask me my programme. I had none. I stayed for a week, then two, and finally lingered on for five weeks. Mulk would not allow me to spend a penny.

Mulk was stocky, full of energy and frothing with ideas. He had a shy chin, a squeaky voice, and was constantly clearing his throat. His habit of speaking incessantly had impaired his vocal cords. I felt like massaging his throat with ghee to smoothen his voice.

I first met him when he visited my house in Lahore. He had just returned from London and was searching for accommodation. Spotting a dingy garage and the broken hut of a sweeper in my compound, he wanted to transform these into a writer's studio. I laughed at the idea. Mulk had a passion to improve the environment, build writers' homes, buy old mansions, occupy ruins, and turn these into creative centres for artists.

His apartment in Bombay faced the sea. Built in the old Parsi style with lots of trees and plants, it had high ceilings, marble flooring and wide double-glazed windows to ward off the torrential monsoons.

This luxury apartment was owned by Anil de Silva, assistant editor of *Marg*, the famous arts magazine. She had oily black hair, a sallow complexion, and was short, vital and graceful. She wore expensive silks in dramatic colour combinations, high-heeled sandals and heavy make-up. Well-versed in Buddhist sculpture, European and Asian art, she had a large personal collection which included George Keyt's paintings of women with enormous musk-melon buttocks.

Mulk would sit at his desk from early morning onwards, dictating articles, messages, letters, and notes. Then a sparse lunch, followed by an hour's rest. A glass of spiced hot tea, and he would go to the *Marg* office. The evenings were set aside for his friends, art exhibitions, dance recitals, foreign visitors and writers. I met some of the leading artists under his roof.

Mulk and Anil often argued over petty sums, as to who spent the money. Where, why, what for? Once, they argued fiercely over half-a-rupee. They sat with their small diaries open, shouting at each other, eyes ablaze. They fought like two sheikhs over the division of a desert kingdom.

They were equal partners not only in bed, but also in

accounts.

I went to see an exhibition of Shivax Chavda's dance paintings at the Taj Hotel. As I walked through the foyer I saw a beautiful woman coming out of a parlour. It was Sakshi. I had met her in Lahore and fallen in love with her at first sight. She was tall, fair-complexioned and voluptuous, and had long black hair cascading down her hips. She wore stylish clothes and glittered at parties.

I had lost trace of her during Partition and often wondered where she was. Had she gone to Bangalore to join her sister? Or been looted and abducted? Where could she be? I had tried to locate her in Delhi but had been unable to find her. Seeing her now, my heart thumped with joy. I told her that I was staying with Mulk Raj Anand. She promised to come and see me the following afternoon.

I waited for her all day, sitting at the window watching the crashing waves of the Arabian Sea ... the sun slowly went down into the flushed waters ... night descended. Thoughts of her gnawed at me. I was under her spell, haunted by her image. She did not come.

A strong sea breeze had been blowing through the window ... I shivered and fell ill. A high temperature. Mulk gave me a thick plaid woollen shirt and ordered me to forget Sakshi.

One day she suddenly appeared and apologised for not being able to come all these days. She had been busy in a legal case with her two sisters over a common inheritance and had been consulting lawyers. Seeing her, all my hurt and anger vanished. I felt her warmth, a caressing sensation which shot through me.

Mulk returned from the office and was happy to find me with Sakshi. He complimented her effusively as he hugged and kissed her.

"Why don't you marry Balwant?" he said. "He is madly in love with you."

"I'm fond of Balwant," she replied. "He is a wonderful man. But I don't love him. If I were to marry him, I would destroy him."

After she left, Mulk snarled, "She is a bitch. Kick her buttocks! Fuck her off! Don't be a sentimental idiot. Go to Europe. Taste French wines! Fuck twenty to thirty wenches. This will heal you of your stupid love. She is selfish. A whore! Good in bed only for some rich bastard."

He continued to curse her, pacing up and down his large room. Then he said, "Come with me to Khandala. Forget her !".

The following day we drove to Khandala, 70 miles away from Bombay, an enchantingly cool spot in the foot-hills of the Ghats.

In the morning I went with Mulk to bathe in a gorge where waterfall roared. He stripped naked, ran, and stood under the fall rubbing his body. I saw glimpses of him through the cascade of water which sparkled like splintered glass. He shouted, "Balwant! Fool! Take off your clothes and join me!"

I stood away because I did not like to bathe naked in the open. Instead, I sauntered up the hill and sat under a tree.

He joined me after his cool shower, and we walked back to the bungalow. It was time for midday meals.

In the evening he took me to the famous Karle caves. We parked the car by the roadside and walked through dry shrubs and a barren sandy terrain to reach the caves. Groups of amorous couples carved in relief adorned the facade. Inside were masterpieces of sculpture chiselled into the giant rock. Rows of pillars on each side, depicting men and women in ecstacy ... the barrel vaulted ceiling receded and multiplied with echoes of eternity ... a breath-taking spectacle. Mulk stood at the opening of the cave and pointed out the details of the Buddhist art and beauty of the human forms.

Suddenly a harsh squeaky sound and the flapping of rubbery wings startled me. A large group of bats detached themselves from the ceiling and flew out of the main entrance in search of their evening meal.

The sky was mottled in orange and dark green. The sun was setting. We trudged back, Mulk walking ahead of me, explaining the history, culture and art of ancient times. I followed him, filled with apprehension at every step lest some wild beast pounce on us from behind. A lone jackal scampered across the path. There was a sense of space, desolation and immense emptiness all around ...

Mulk threw a small cocktail party in honour of Ilya Ehrenburg, the famous Soviet novelist. Present were the poet Ali Sardar Jafri, Urdu writers Krishen Chander and Rajinder Singh Bedi, the wealthy leftist intellectual Romesh Thapar, his wife Raj, and some painters and poets. All of us adored Ehrenburg and were under his spell. We had read his novels and the despatches he had sent from the war front. He had inspired millions of readers and battalions of Soviet soldiers to fight against Hitler's army for world peace.

Mulk had invited Roshan Vajifdar, a beautiful classical

dancer, to give a twenty-minute performance of Bharata Natyam to entertain and educate our distinguished guest. She hated being paraded before dignitaries, and had agreed only after much persuasion. Through the magic of her dance she created immense space in that small area, her long arms flying over our heads, her eyes transmitting magical *bhavas*. Ehrenburg was greatly moved.

Mulk served wine. Everyone toasted Ehrenburg's health and world peace.

The front door flew open and Frank Moraes walked in, arm in arm with a woman, holding a bottle of wine in his hand. Every one stood up to greet the Chief Editor of *The Times of India*. Mulk introduced him to Ehrenburg, and requested him to join us for a drink.

Frank was a fearless critic of sham and loved exposing political and social corruption. He was appalled by the Moscow purges in 1936, the liquidation of top party leaders like Bukharin, and by the thousands of people who had been sent to Siberia for hard labour, where they died of hunger and the bitter cold.

He drew himself up in front of Ehrenburg and asked him, "Do you know about the massacre of labourers in Siberia? Workers who had dug their own graves and rolled themselves down into those death pits. Do you know about that?"

"No", replied Ehrenburg.

"Do you know about the false trial of Jewish doctors?"

"No."

"You are a liar !"

Frank's words stunned the group. Ehrenburg looked embarrassed, gave a sardonic smile, and started sucking on his pipe.

Frank was in a rage. Pointing his finger at Ehrenburg, he

thundered, "How can a Jewish intellectual like you not know the facts? You were in the inner Party circle. Stalin's friend. You are dishonest. A liar!"

Mulk and Jafri tried to stop Frank but he pushed them aside. "It's not a question of being polite. It's a question of speaking the truth. You are all pigs, squealing about peace movements. Bullshit ! Toasting peace ... All of you have been bought over. You cannot face the truth !"

He left with the woman, the bottle of wine tucked under his arm.

Mulk apologized to Ehrenburg, "Please don't mind him. He is drunk!"

2

Three women—Litto, Perin and Vimla—all Communist Party activists, had occupied my room in my absence and set up their typewriters. When I entered they did not notice me, and kept pounding at the keys, typing sheets of paper with a fierce speed. They were on a crusade.

I looked around. The walls of my room were plastered with posters of the Berlin Youth Festival. Stacks of cyclostyled papers, literature, and magazines littered the floor.

The women wore their hair severely swept back, rolled into buns. They had a moral arrogance. They were yoginis, above sexual or worldly temptations, committed to their revolutionary cause.

Becoming aware of my presence, they looked up. Fair-complexioned Litto, who had the innocence of a teenager, said, "We are sorry to have taken over your house. But we had no other choice. Nobody would give us accommodation on rent, and our work was urgent. We'll be here for one more day, and then pack up."

After two days they wound up and disappeared, leaving behind one large poster on the wall.

I stared at the poster. Youths of five continents — white, brown, yellow, swarthy, black — dancing hand in hand. It was the biggest cultural rally of the world youth, marching, dancing, singing, hugging, kissing and celebrating the joy of life.

I was asked by the organisers to go to this festival, but I needed a passport. I applied for one. The Indian Government delayed the matter. Hoping to speed up the process, I went to Patiala, where the Chief Minister was my friend. I filled up the forms and gave them to him.

The following day he told me that he could not issue me a passport because I was on a list of five hundred "anti-government progressives" barred from going abroad. I could not believe it. What had I done to be on this list? I returned to Delhi and applied once again. The Home Secretary told me the same thing. I met some Members of Parliament and asked them to intervene. How could I be refused a passport—my birth right? My application was lost in the maze. It was Kafka's *Castle*.

Finally I was told that the only person who could clear my file was the Chief of Police H.K. Handoo, the right-hand man of Prime Minister Nehru. Through some contacts I reached him, and was given an appointment at his residence. A tall handsome man with white hair, he was graceful and polite. He gave me a cup of tea and said, "It is no crime to be a progressive. Many communist leaders have been given a passport. Why not you? I will look into the matter." He advised me to apply again, and said that there would be no problem. But I was hitting my head against a blind wall. My application was rejected again, without any reason. Confused, tortured and helpless, I felt trapped in my own country.

Why was Nehru's government not allowing me to go out of the country to see the world? Nehru himself had been educated in England, had waged a war of freedom against the British, and championed the freedom of movement and speech. Why, then, was I being shut in?

Again and again the question rose in my head: Why? ... Why?

During my student days in Lahore I had been arrested in Mahatma Gandhi's Quit India movement. The police were after my friend Tara Chand Gupta, who hid his identity by wearing a tilted felt hat and dark sunglasses. Ironically, the police were searching for a man of this very description.

Tara Chand was an active member of an underground revolutionary party, and used to camp sometimes with Miss Florence, a young missionary school teacher who was ignorant of his political activities. One night I went to see him off at Florence's small bungalow. The police had laid a trap and had been waiting for him for three days. They swooped down on us. Someone yelled gleefully, "We have a new shikar", and a tall gruff man, his teeth glinting through his thick black moustache, arrested me along with Tara Chand. I felt the icy chill of iron handcuffs and heard the long rattling chain.

They put me in the Mozang thana lock-up. The constable marched me down a poorly-lit corridor, threw an old woollen blanket into a cell, and pointed to a dirty bed on the floor, "Lie there!"

I covered myself with the moth-eaten blanket, its holes winking like stars ... I thought of the prisoners who had breathed into this blanket ... their foul breath ... may be suffering from syphilis or tuberculosis ... their consumptive vapours ... their stink ... I slept heavily, drugged with the smell of urine and the blanket.

I woke up late in the afternoon. Joginder Singh, the thana sub-inspector, stood across the bars, staring at me. He wore a plumed khaki turban, had shining narrow eyes, and a golden beard. I asked him how long would they keep me in the lock-up. He laughed, "Afraid of jail, babu ji? Lost your courage so soon?"

"I just want to know how long you will keep me here. Six days, six months, or six years. ..?"

"The Government never tells anyone that. Nobody knows. Neither I, nor *Laat* Saheb. Only Hitler knows it, or your Gandhi. Why are you so anxious to know?"

"I want to work out my programme."

"What programme?"

"My programme to keep myself happy in this stinking cell!"

I organised my schedule in a manner to kill time: day-dreaming ... pacing up and down ... sleeping ... staring at the ceiling ... counting its beams, walls, cracks, blotches ...

I would lie half-asleep, listening to the dull murmur of the prison, and suddenly wake up and feel a spurt of energy. Clutching the iron bars, I would press my face against them to get a glimpse of the outside world .... the blur of a wheel ... a slice of sky ... a fluttering saree ... the head of a running horse ...

My friends Navtej Singh, Inderjit Singh and Lal Chand came to see me. We lived in the same lodge, eating, playing and studying together, and used to have long discussions on the war, films, Gandhi and Stalin. They brought some books, shirts, a tooth brush, a cake of Pear's soap, and a blanket, and promised to return in the evening with spiced hot food prepared by Marshal Budenny. Navtej always referred to our cook by this name because of his strong jaw and handlebar moustache.

The Soviet Marshal was repulsing enemy forces, conquering battles. So was our cook. He would slap chapattis and hurl them into the blazing oven, pull them out, and throw them onto our plates. His sorties earned him this title. If any of us left a half-nibbled morsel on the plate, his eyeballs would bulge.

That evening I waited for my friends. It was biting cold ... the 5th of February 1943 ... the festival of Basant Panchami ... Mahatma Gandhi was in jail and had started his fast unto death. I heard a song from a nearby pandal: *"Ai Gandhi jeetay rehna, jub tuk swaraj paoon"*. (Oh Gandhi, keep living till we achieve freedom.) This doggerel blared on the loudspeaker.

It was interspersed with the chanting and singing of a *kirtan* from a nearby gurudwara. Gandhi's song and Guru's *baani* mingled in the air and floated to me as I stood gripping the bars, waiting for my friends. I saw some people enter with blankets wrapped around them. As they breathed out, their breath turned to fog. The bitter cold of Lahore chilled my bones. I listened to every footfall, watched every person entering the police station. My friends did not show up.

What could have happened? Were they afraid of the police, lest their names be associated with Gandhi's movement? Then why had they promised to come? I was filled with anguish. I did not want to believe that my friends would drop me just like that. I was jolted out of my reverie when a Sikh devotee from the gurudwara came with hot *puris* and *halwa* for prisoners.

Joginder Singh stood outside my cell and said, "Babuji,

it's past eleven. The moon has set in the sky. Receive the *karah prasad*."

I received the hot *halwa* in both hands and enjoyed each morsel ... delicious ... unforgettable.

Joginder Singh lived in a quarter within the compound of the police station. When off duty at night, he would remove his turban and coil his long hair which nestled like a cobra in thick yellow grass. He would ask me questions about my village and student life. He felt great pity for me and would ask if I needed anything.

One night, Joginder emerged from behind the barracks. He wore a loose kurta and a striped *tehmad,* his long silken hair coiled on his head. He stood near the main gate and started singing a film song in a heart-rending voice: *duniya mein gharibon ko aaraam nahin milta* (The poor in this world know no rest). His soulful voice resounded and charged the air with pathos, expressing the misery and torture of the poor. His face softened, and his became the voice of the downtrodden, pouring out their sorrows.

Suddenly he stopped singing and shouted at a bullock cart passing by on the road, loaded with sugarcane. The lantern dangling under the cart was not lit. He roared, "Grab that *haramzada* ! Bring him here !"

A constable ran out and dragged the cart-driver in. Joginder kicked him. "Mother-fucker ! Don't you know the law? Going on the road without a light? Is it your father's road? Or your mother's?" He slapped the driver, who fell on the ground howling. "*Sarkar! huzoor!* Pardon me !"

Joginder yelled, "Pig ! Pull out a bundle of sugarcane from the cart. Let me see if the sugarcane tastes sweet. Otherwise I'll push the cane up your ass !"

The driver went out, wiping his tears with his shirt sleeve, and returned with a bundle of juicy sugarcane. Joginder distributed these to his staff and presented one to me. He turned to the driver, "Disappear, you mother-fucker!" He grabbed him by the neck and gave him a kick which sent him staggering away.

After a generous distribution of the booty, Joginder Singh resumed his song, "The poor in this world know no rest." His voice was filled with pain. A tragic sensation raced through my body, stirring the depths of my soul, a cathartic experience transforming me.

One day Joginder came to my cell and asked me if I would like to have tea with him. He ordered the constable to open the iron gate and led me out to a bench under a tree. After serving me with sugared tea, he said, "You are free. There's no case against you."

The constable packed my books, rolled my bedding and put these in a horse-driven tonga. "Good luck!" said Joginder. He shook hands with me and saw me off.

I came out in the street and saw the bustling shops, the people, the sky. I could not believe it. Just walking on the road, riding a tonga was a miracle. Everything looked so beautiful.

After this incident, my name was put on a police list of "anti-government progressives". Years later, when the British left, the Indian Government inherited all their bureaucratic files and police records, unchanged.

Everytime I applied for a passport, they would look up my police record, where I was still listed as a "dangerous revolutionary!"

Ali Sardar Jafri came to Delhi and stayed with me. He was tall, slim, and had a handsome sun-burnt face with a mop of thick wavy hair. While he recited poems his wayward hair would fall on his cheeks and he would flick it back, which added charm to his personality.

Burning with revolutionary zeal, he championed socialist realism and wrote poems which swayed the masses and influenced hundreds of poets. Arguing about the function of poetry, he said, "A poet is a prophet. We are prophets of the new world!"

For his firebrand poems, he was imprisoned along with other revolutionaries in Salem jail. While demonstrating, they were fired upon. Some were killed. Jafri survived.

Discussions on art and literature continued in my house till late at night. "The Urdu *ghazal* evokes only delicate and complex sentiments of love, beauty, and yearning—like a *haiku*—and cannot carry the load of a sustained thought-process," Jafri argued. "Only a rhyme-free poem can. If an idea is reactionary, however good the form, the poem will be third rate. If the idea is good, it will evolve its own form. Idea is the thing!"

I hit back. "Nonsense! What is the idea behind a pair of shoes? Or sunflowers? But Van Gogh made them immortal. It was the power of his brush which lent universal meaning to the idea. What's the idea behind the *alaap* of a *raga*? Or a sitar recital of Ravi Shankar? Nothing! Any idea becomes great when touched by a master."

Jafri lost his temper. "You are a pucca reactionary. You worship the form, I the idea."

One late evening as we returned from a Chinese dinner, he talked about Chinese poets, writers, and the revolution sweeping over the Himalayas. He quoted Mao's Red Book to me. I spoke of Iqbal's poetry and its magical effect. "You have criticised Iqbal and written articles against him," I said to him.

"But Iqbal is great ... I am not a Muslim. I don't believe in Allah or Satan or Karbala or Hejaz. Why does Iqbal move me? Something enters my blood ... brings tears to my eyes ... when he describes the power of Muslims ... the flashing sword of Islam ... their conquests ... I am moved to the depth of my soul. Why?"

"Wherever his content is poor, his poetry is poor, "Jafri replied. He quoted two couplets of Iqbal which glorified the concept of superman, written in praise of Kemal Ataturk, a despot..

"These couplets could apply to Shakespeare, Kalidasa, Guru Nanak, Buddha ... " I replied. "Why do you limit these lines only to Ataturk, who I think was great anyway!"

We argued and argued. Like a rudderless boat the argument drifted around the same point.

Deep in my soul I felt darkness and confusion. My writing was a mechanical justification of the working class and a blind condemnation of the rich. I wrote some of my worst plays during this period. The Progressive Writers' Movement gave me social enlightenment and knowledge of the classes, but blurred my creative thinking. My bad plays, like *The Dove*, *The Landlord*, and *The Water Sluice* were being staged in rural gatherings and their rave reviews published in leading papers. It was absurd.

Rajinder Singh Bedi and I made many rounds to All India Radio for a job. We would sit outside the Director's room waiting to be called in. But the Director always had either a bad cold, a bad schedule or a bad temper.

Bedi said to me, "I am going to try my luck in Bombay. Here I am denied a job because I am an Urdu writer. And you because you are a Punjabi writer. To top it all, we are progressives. Every government is afraid of the word 'progressive'. Even Stalin hates it. In Russia it means democracy, and in the democratic world it means communism. It's a doomed word!"

On the third day Bedi and his wife came to my house to discuss their plans. His wife said, "He is going to Bombay. What will he do there? We have only fifteen hundred rupees. He is taking one thousand with him. He will blow it up in a week. How will we eat?" But Bedi soothed her. "If I sit here this money will evaporate in two months anyway. Let me try luck."

He left for Bombay. There he hired a small hotel room and started writing for films. He had a number of friends who were now directors and respected his writings. Bedi's dialogues were a great success and he became a star writer.

When the Communist Party of India became respectable after Khrushchev's visit to India in the mid-fifties, AIR opened its gates to the progressives. Bedi received a letter from All India Radio requesting him to write a play for them. Bedi replied, "I have blacklisted AIR from my programme!"

In the summer my room used to become an oven due to the blazing sun. It had only one little window, and no cross-ventilation. I would go out and sit in the Coffee House where the air was heavy with steamy fumes and the perspiration of customers, but it was still better than being in my cell.

I fell ill. I had not known illness for years, had never taken any pills or vitamins. Natural urges kept the body energetic like a jungle animal—eating, sleeping, working, wandering.

Now in illness, my body burning, I did not know who to reach. As I lay in bed, my temperature would shoot up and slowly come down, and again rise. I could not sleep at night. I had no money. The idea of a doctor frightened me. He could charge any amount, and may fleece me. I might die ... People in

Delhi died all the time. My publisher owned me money, and had been putting me off with promises for the past two years. Why didn't he pay me my money? If he didn't, I might die ...

I sent for a friend who brought some medicines from a chemist. I swallowed the pills, one every four hours. My head spun and I lay in semi-consciousness ... my pillow wet with perspiration. My body fought its battle. The temperature fell and I slowly recovered, full of anger and bitterness against the publisher.

Five affluent Sardars had pooled money and set up a publishing house, with Mubarak Singh as the Managing Director. It was flooded with orders, but due to mismanagement did not make any profits.

Mubarak Singh, a socio-political personality of Amritsar, had gentle eyes, cheerful teeth, and a short wavy steel-grey beard. He wore a homespun khaddar turban and a khaddar shirt. His right foot was encased in a specially manufactured crooked leather shoe, as he was club-footed. He was a connoisseur of arts and music, and a lover of dogs.

After I recovered from my illness I went to Amritsar and asked him for money. He reeled out a long list of his financial woes.

Pulling at his beard, he said, "I'm always fighting a wrong battle for a right cause. Life has been like this. Temptations ... Now I am the President of the Municipal Committee. Its annual budget is thirty million rupees. But myself, I don't have a penny."

"But people say you have millions in your bank."

He smiled, "I wish I had. One needs guts to take bribes. ... I don't have the courage. I am a coward. I have no bank balance. I even borrowed money for milk for my dog."

"You are worried about your dog, and not about me?" I

snapped. He laughed, "You have no idea of the devotion of a dog. I can starve myself but not my dog. He is loyal. He cannot speak, but his beautiful eyes and face speak a million words. I cannot starve him."

I returned to Delhi disappointed, cheated, angry, and helpless. I sent him letters, telegrams, even a legal notice, but received no money. Finally, I filed a lawsuit against him.

His lawyer filed a reply, stating that I had not written a book, that I did not know English, and was a poor Punjabi writer of no consequence. They owed me no money.

This infuriated me. What the lawyer had said in defence was a white lie. I had a statement of account of my royalty. How could Mubarak Singh deny that?

One morning Mubarak Singh turned up at my house with a little handbag, his face tense. He was to appear in court against me that day.

He sat staring at me, stroking his beard. "I never believed that you would drag me to court. Shocking. For the sake of money .. I can't believe it...".

"I have nothing to say to you, Mubarak." I said coldly. "I will see you in court!"

His face turned purple, the colour travelling from his beard to his eyes. He got up and walked out in anger.

We both appeared before the judge. I was dying to hear from Mubarak Singh under oath that he owed me nothing. In fact, I was secretly wishing that he would tell this blatant lie so that I could enjoy it perversely. "Don't be emotional, or you will lose the case," my lawyer warned me. "Mubarak Singh has already declared in his written statement that he owes you nothing."

I surged forward to ask him the question but court procedure did not allow it. I had to speak through my lawyer. The two lawyers went into a long argument over some technical point. Finally I burst out, "Your Honour! Just let Mubarak Singh say in your presence that he owes me nothing. I will accept it as the truth and withdraw the case!"

Mubarak Singh was taken aback. He tugged at his beard for a while and said, "Your Honour, what Gargi claims is true. I do owe him the amount."

I won the case but did not have the heart to claim the money. Mubarak came to pay the first instalment. After that I forgot about the remaining payments. We became good friends again.

Sakshi was in town. My heart started beating fast when I learnt it. Mulk's advice melted like ice cubes in boiling water. I was possessed by her. If I saw a loosely rolled mass of black hair streaming down a woman's back I thought it was she.

I telephoned her. The same husky voice, breathing desire into me through mysterious subterranean telephonic coils ... her breath ... so physical, so passion-charged.

She promised to come the following day, but did not show up. This aggravated my hunger for her. I telephoned her again and again but her maidservant always said, "Mem saheb has gone out." She did not know when she would be back. Always the same reply.

Evening fell. Shadows deepened. The moon rose from behind the champak tree and cast pale smudges in my courtyard.

I spread my bed on the large wooden divan outside and slept. Possessed by her image, I dreamt of her voluptuous form. I sent her psychic waves ... telepathic currents so that she could understand my torture.

I saw images ... her mass of black hair swishing over my face ... sea waves rippling like a silk saree ... boats ... tall trees swaying in wind ... a horse running ... the clatter of hooves ...

Someone was knocking on the door of the courtyard. I woke up. The full moon shone in the sky. I looked around and listened. Again, a knock. I opened the door.

Sakshi stood there in a loose cotton kurta and night pyjamas, her white convertible Studebaker parked to one side.

She closed the door and walked into the courtyard. Was it a dream or reality? How could she come at midnight?

She said, "I knew you were waiting for me. I have been feeling very guilty all these days. I'm very silly."

She lay down on the divan and said, "Let's sleep."

I held her and inhaled the fragrance of her hair. She unbuttoned her shirt and released her enormous silken breasts ... luscious, smelling of honey and roses ... the moonlight fell on us ... a milky cascade from the sky ... magical rays ... Bathed in full moonlight she looked like a marble sculpture.

The courtyard heaved with passion. The champak buds, awakened by the touch of moonlight opened in full bloom and exhaled a delicious perfume ... the seductive fragrance of desire. Then everything became still .... only her heavings ... I sat hypnotised by her beauty ... a goddess of love.

A mad desire welled up in me to hold her ... kiss her again and again ... drink at her fragrant dark-nippled breasts. I bent over her and started kissing her. Suddenly I realised that she was fast asleep, her half-open lips shining in the moonlight. As I lay there looking at her, she opened her eyes, looked around, and sat up. "What's the time? Must be past three. It's late. I must go."

I begged her to stay, but she was in a great hurry. She quickly looped her long wild hair, buttoned her shirt, and walked out. I heard the door bang and the Studebaker racing away.

Later, I learnt that she had a violent quarrel that night with her lover, a rich young industrialist. He had been drinking heavily and would not stop. She broke the bottle and he slapped her. Mad with rage, she had walked out and jumped into her car, driving around aimlessly while her distraught lover searched for her frantically. On an impulse she had landed in my courtyard.

After that night, my relationship with her became platonic.

3

Pablo Neruda had flown from Paris as "ambassador" of the World Peace Council to meet Indian writers and artists.

This man was different from the image I had formed of him by reading his poems of blood, passion, anguish, and love in surrealistic flashes. I had imagined him to be a slim Chilean. But he was portly, and dressed like a senator in a dark grey suit. What I remembered most about him is his large baby-face and droopy eyes. A dreamy, swooning look, as if disinterested in everything around him.

On the jacket cover of a book of his earlier poems was scrawled his name in thick black ink, as if by a child. The poems had unusual imagery: injured iron ... murdered tomatoes ... cheeks of salt ... tongue like a red arrow ... twisted chairs waiting for winter ... roses of the lonely ocean and broken waters ... fish with bloodstained teeth in search of emeralds ... the ship's dead covered with masculine poppies. These images haunted me, and gave me a fresh vision of contemporary poetry ... in some ways his was extension of Garcia Lorca's poetic genius.

Neruda's inner eye was sharper than his outer eye. Once, the Peruvian writers had held a function in his honour. After a heavy lunch and wine, his hosts insisted upon showing him the ruins of Macchu Picchu, the site of ancient Incan city, about 7000 feet above sea level in the Andes. Sleepy and reluctant, Neruda went up the towering height just to oblige the Peruvian writers. Exhausted, perspiring, he hardly seemed to see anything. But he wrote a magnificent poem describing the ancient rocks carved by torrents, furrowed and glazed by time, at places levelled by Nature's sharp knife.

No Peruvian could have written such a poem.

At a luncheon with Pandit Nehru, Neruda handed him a sealed letter from Juliot-Curie, the French Nobel Laureate scientist who in his letter had advocated the urgency of the World Peace Movement. Neruda tried to sell the "Peace" idea, but Nehru did not buy it. This hurt Neruda. The police had been shadowing him. Customs officials in Bombay had clawed at his suitcase, going through every seam of his clothes, books, papers, private notebooks, even socks and underwear. He had not expected this cold welcome. At the writers' meeting that evening, he referred to this incident. He did not talk much, only looked at us with his heavy-lidded eyes. We had all read his poems on peace ... peace for farmers, vineyards, lakes, beautiful women, and for the embroidered pillow on which a child sleeps.

These poems were like Picasso's 'Dove' which, in fact, was a hurriedly-sketched pigeon.

Louis Aragon (famous for his "Love Songs to Elsa") had

gone to Picasso and conveyed to him that the Party wanted him to paint a Peace Dove. Picasso was furious at such a command. Aragon begged him, saying that it was a matter of the Party's honour, as he had already announced it in his weekly *Lettres Francaises*.

During those days Picasso had been drawing a series of pigeons in various moods, but was not satisfied with them. His room was littered with these sketches. Picking up a discarded "pigeon," he asked Aragon, "Will this do?" Aragon grabbed the sketch, ran out and published it in his weekly. The pigeon flew all over the world as a "Peace Dove."

Neruda, too, turned out tons of peace songs to serve the socialist cause. Indian poets—from Ali Sardar Jafri to Sahir to Akhtar to Faiz to Punjabi poets in villages—copied Neruda's imagery.

I very much wanted to meet Neruda again, but he had no time.

I was surprised when the very next day he visited my house. He entered the courtyard with his wife, a shrivelled old woman. She looked like his mother. The Punjabi writer Navtej Singh had conducted them to my little house because they wanted to see how an Indian writer lived.

Neruda introduced me to his wife. I welcomed them into my room. He looked at the walls, at her, at me, his eyes travelling listlessly. He seemed bored. Between awkward silences, his wife carried on a broken conversation and smiled twice or thrice. Her teeth looked false, dull and lusterless. Like a skull.

Suddenly I thought of giving her a gift. I took out a hand-spun red shawl with silver moons embroidered on it, and explained that when a bride first visits a house she is always given a gift. She opened the shawl and exclaimed "Beautiful!" but did not know how to wear it. Neruda took the shawl and draped it around her head.

"My bride," he said. She smiled. Her yellowed teeth made me think of death.

He kissed her on her lips.

I had a copy of his book and wanted him to autograph it. He thumbed through its pages. On the left side was Spanish, and on the right English, almost word for word.

"There are some mistakes in it," he said, and took out his pen and corrected them. I kept the book as a souvenir.

After he had gone, I kept thinking about his relationship with his wife-mother.

He had left his first love, Josie Bliss, "a kind of Burmese panther", as he called her. Her blood boiling with jealousy, she would hover around his bed at night, brandishing a sharp long knife, perhaps to kill him. After violent scenes of blazing hate, they parted. Neruda wrote *Widower's Tango*, a sad brooding poem in memory of this woman, without whom he felt lost and lonely.

Now he was with this woman — Delia del Corril — old, skinny, passionless.

I wondered how he could live with her. How could he love her? A man raised among ripe oranges and grapes and the sunny beaches of Chile. Was it some revolutionary obligation binding him to her? He worshipped beauty and sensuality. This woman had none. Why did he carry the burden of this lizard ...?

I wished he would leave her!

4

One day my name was suddenly cleared by the Home Ministry. It had been done at the intervention of Doctor Baliga, President of the Indo-Soviet Cultural Society. He was Pandit Nehru's personal physician, and used to fly from Bombay to New Delhi whenever Nehru was indisposed. He would breeze into Nehru's bedroom, give a profound wink and pat his back. "Nothing wrong with you, Panditji ! You are in perfect health. Don't worry! I am here." Nehru would feel half his illness vanish. Baliga had sent him a list of 35 "dangerous leftists" to be cleared for a visit to the Soviet Union. Nehru okayed it without question.

I left for Moscow.

I stayed there for two months and saw superb productions

of Chekhov, Gorky, Tolstoy, Turgenev, Ostrovsky and Gogol, as well as Shakespeare, Shaw, Ibsen and modern Soviet writers. Every day two plays, an opera, or a ballet in the gilded Bolshoi.

My interpreter, Effonina Alexanderovna, a school teacher of English and instant translator, would whisper dialogues into my ear so that it did not disturb the audience. She wore a high fur cap strapped around her chin, and a heavy fur coat. Proud of Russia's heritage, she fed me with her knowledge of history, music, visual arts, and took me to rehearsals of Moscow Art Theatre—the Mecca of actors.

It was the opening night of a fresh production of Chekhov's *The Sea Gull*. The play had first been staged at Petrograd in 1896, and had failed miserably. Chekhov fled from the theatre, announcing that he was no playwright. Two years later, after Stanislavsky's sensitive production, *The Sea Gull* became a symbol of Moscow Art Theatre, the insignia painted on its drop curtain, souvenirs, brochures, chairs, and ushers' uniforms. It started a new era in world theatre history.

Effonina guided me through the slushy streets. Snow had been falling all night, but had now stopped. It was biting cold. Young Russian girls eating *maroyani* (ice cream) were rushing to the theatre.

Entering the foyer, we felt gusts of warm air and regained our breath. Women were handing over their fur coats to cloakroom assistants and hurriedly combing their hair and freshening their lips in front of large gilded mirrors. We went into the theatre and sat down.

The curtain went up. Hushed silence. On stage, a distant lake with shrubs and trees shimmered as a large golden moon appeared on the horizon.

Effonina nudged me, "Do you know the woman sitting in the second row?"

In front of us sat a shrivelled old woman in a black dress with black kid gloves and a white-fringed black velvet cap.

"Who is she?" I asked.

"Olga Knipper-Chekhova," she whispered.

My heart missed a beat.

It was Anton Chekhov's wife. She had played the role of Arkadina in *The Sea Gull* in 1898.

Effonina bent forward, "*Puzavasta ... aadin minoot ...*"

Olga turned her face. Her beady eyes glimmered. Her face was a web of thin wrinkles. Effonina introduced me to her. The woman gave a faint smile. She rested her silver-knobbed stick by her side, extended her hand, and tried to peel off her glove. "Please don't remove your glove," I said. "I'll kiss it." But I then changed my mind and requested her to remove her glove. I held her thin pale hand and planted a kiss on it, thinking that Anton Chekhov must have kissed this very hand on this very spot hundreds of times. His kisses were alive on her hand ... pulsations ... transmitting Chekhov's breath ... memories in live cells ... a rich heritage suspended in time.

A serpentine queue of people slithered in the snow towards the mausoleum of Lenin and Stalin. The two leaders lay embalmed in glass cases in a vault in the Kremlin. Ali Sardar Jafri, Khwaja Ahmed Abbas and I, being State guests, were conducted straight to a little marble door flanked by two tall, stiff Russian soldiers. They stood like statues, frozen with devotion, guarding the mummies more precious than the Czar's treasure of gold and jewels. No cameras were allowed inside.

We entered the vault and circled the transparent tombs, looking at the two leaders lying in State, mummified by expert

Russian scientists. Originally, Lenin's tomb had been in the centre of the sanctum sanctorum. But Stalin ordered the tomb to be shifted to one side to make place for him to lie parallel to Lenin when his time came. His wish was honoured. The two giants were united in their last journey. Peasants, workers, old men, youths and schoolboys visited the mausoleum, their faces lit with wonder at seeing their beloved leaders in their original physical form.

In the hushed breathing of pilgrims, I was struck by a sinister feeling, astonishment, fear creeping in my bones. I thought of human nature and man's lust for eternity.

During those days a daring French journalist had hidden a tiny camera with electronic gadgets in his coat pocket and taken a photograph of Stalin and Lenin lying in their glass cases. It was like stealing the Golden Fleece. He sold the picture to the glossy *Paris Match* at a fabulous price, and it was splashed as a centre spread—the heads of the two leaders in a halo of light, the rest of their bodies merging into darkness. The picture sent shudders through the Soviet body politic. How had the enemy penetrated the sacred vault? The security guards were dismissed and sent to Siberia.

Later Stalin, dubbed a ruthless tyrant, was removed and buried near the side wall of the Kremlin. Lenin was shifted back to the centre, to lie there as an object of worship and faith, a symbol of inspiration.

An aura of chilling power emanated from the pink walled fort over which the Red Star shone high on a steeple. By its side stood the multi-coloured onion-domed cathedral of Saint Basil. The Red Square did not look large. It appeared no larger than a cricket field, one-tenth of the vast spacious parade ground of India Gate. But its image loomed frighteningly large in the mind of the world. During the Czarist rule criminals had been brought in front of the cathedral and their heads chopped off. Red blood flowed. Now the Red Square was a square of peace, fraternity, and happiness.

As we emerged from the vault, a biting cold wind was blowing, raking up snowflakes. Houses sat in the snow like shivering black bulls.

I was invited for lunch at the dacha of a famous writer. We drove for an hour on icy roads, the fields covered with a chalk-white carpet. The driver wore a Mongol leather cap, and his thin veins stood out on his cracked ruddy face.

Throughout our journey Effonina angrily ordered and rebuked him, and he argued back. I did not understand what they were arguing about. Effonina would turn to me with a smile every now and then and explain to me the cultural background of some building or mausoleum flying past.

On reaching the dacha, the wife of our host hugged us. She was a large woman with streaks of grey hair and puckered lips and was wearing a faded long woollen skirt. She was a heart surgeon. Her twenty-two-year old daughter Natasha was a civil engineer.

The lunch started ceremoniously with vodka, a toast to India, red caviar sandwiches which were to be quickly munched after a gulp of vodka. The meal consisted of borscht, lobster salad and roast lamb. Pale sunlight filtered through the amber window-glass and warmed us as we sat discussing heart transplantation and theatre.

"I love music and embroidery," Natasha said, "I have knitted a pullover with a new design in the latest Paris fashion!"

I thought she was joking. France and the Soviet Union were locked in a cold war. Everything French was hated. Maupassant was banned. So was Picasso's art—except his Peace Dove, and a few politicized paintings. The French language, literature, nudes and fashions were an insult to the socialist order.

Natasha returned with a half-knitted pullover and a 1953 *Vogue* magazine which displayed the new fashions of knitwear worn by Paris models.

"I have copied the design from *Vogue*. The first eight pages have been torn out so that customs do not detect it."

I wondered at how the latest Paris designs, like underground literature, were smuggled into Russia, surfacing in far-off rural houses. The youth were hungrily absorbing, copying, storing and hiding these in their chests.

Effonina was not happy with my visits to the Baku Restaurant, where Azerbaijanis played music on the rabab as men ate hot spicy lamb curry and *romali roti*. "This is not a good place," she said. "People here are rowdy. They fight and yell at one another while eating."

She also did not have a high opinion of the Gypsy Theatre. "It's plebian, noisy, and sentimental, full of dance and song. No realism. No artistic merit. It doesn't have the soul-stirring effect of Moscow Art Theatre."

The word 'soul' stuck in my memory. I had met Elizabeth Hapgood, translator of Stanislavsky's works, in New York in 1962. She had invited him to work on his *An Actor Prepares* in her villa in the south of France, which had the warm southern climate so essential for his failing health. She would sit with him going over each word. Stanislavsky complained to her that in his original text he had used the expression 'The soul of an actor', but the Moscow publishers had removed the word 'soul' and substituted it with 'mind'. This grieved him very much.

I went to see the much-publicized play *Aza* in the Gypsy Theatre. It is the story of a gypsy girl who falls in love with a stranger. Tragedy strikes when the chief of the clan does not allow them to marry. The love-striken Aza departs with the caravan, the lover following her.

Olga Petrova, a beautiful gypsy dancer, played Aza. She danced wildly, flourishing her many-layered gauze skirt, kicking and stomping in fierce rythms, climaxing her dance with breast shudders. The audience broke into thunderous applause, whistling and cat-calling. I saw *Aza* three times and every time felt the same thrill and ecstacy. *Aza* had echoes of the colour and rhythms of Rajasthan's desert music. The actors were open, laughed loudly, and used expansive gestures. Some gypsy words were similar to those in Punjabi and Rajasthani : *kann* (ear), *supp* (snake), *dudh* (milk), *nukk* (nose) *rutt* (blood) and *ikk-doe-trai* (one-two-three).

Barkan, director of the Gypsy Theatre, commissioned me to write a play for them and promised that Olga would play the heroine. After my return to Delhi I finished the song-dance drama *Sohini Mahiwal* and sent it to Barkan. The play was the story of Mirza Izzat Baig, a young merchant from Bokhara who travelled to India and camped in Gujrat by the Chenab river (now in Pakistan) and fell in love with the beautiful Sohini, the daughter of a potter. It was in the Romeo-Juliet mold, similar to the love stories of Indian films, and ended in the twin deaths of the lovers.

Barkan mounted the production and invited me to see it.

Olga played Sohini. After the performance the gypsy players raised their wine-filled horns and toasted me and Olga. She gave a quick dance in my honour as women clapped and uttered groans of 'hoo, hoo' in ecstasy. The play is still in their repertoire.

When I visited Moscow in 1974, they were rehearsing some other play. I asked for Olga Petrova. She had walked off on hearing that I was coming, and refused to see me. She thought she was not as beautiful now as she was in the role of Sohini in 1959, and did not want to ruin her image.

Years later, I heard that the Gypsy Theatre was visiting New Delhi and performing at Kamani. I went to see their performance. Their singing was modernised and did not have the blood-stirring groans and sparkle.

But when they danced, they were superb. A fat woman was dancing in exciting rhythms ... eddies of passion, like a golden river in flood. She broke into a high-pitched quivering yell which whipped fever in my veins as she danced clicking her fingers, ending in breast-shudders.

I went backstage to meet the new director (Barkan was no more), and asked him if Olga had come with the troupe. The fat dancer came up to me and smiled through her brownish-yellow teeth. 'I am Olga!'

I was staying at the Hotel Ukrainiya, a newly built 35-storey X-mas cake. Habib Tanvir, a young theatre director from Delhi, was also staying in this hotel. We had met after two years.

Habib was known as a lady killer in those days. Women could not resist his charms. He had countless escapades.

One of the love-smitten girls was Svetlana, a nineteen-year beauty with silky auburn hair and royal blue eyes. She was an elevator girl in the hotel. Russia had overhauled its hotel staff, specially the counter girls, receptionists, interpreters and elevator operators. Earlier, fat babushkas had hand-operated rusty cages which slowly moved up and down. Now they had slick, push-button telephone-fitted elevators.

One day Svetlana stopped the lift mid-way when she found me alone. She begged me to help her meet Habib (whom she called Khabeeb), and explained to me by gestures and in broken Russian that she wanted to go out with him with a bottle of wine by the riverside and sing and roll on the grass in moonlight. She would bring a friend for me and we would be a foursome.

I narrated this to Habib. He disapproved of the dangerous game lest the police arrest us. But Svetlana did not care. She was pure passion. She was the Nina, the Olga, the Anya and Varya of Chekhov, sighing for life, consumed by passion. She prowled about the hotel, searching for Habib from elevator to elevator, desire burning in her royal-blue eyes.

But Habib was not to be found.

Habib and I often went to see plays together and returned late to our hotel. The main restaurants were closed by 11 o'clock. Only one cafe on the roof top served a meagre menu till midnight. From this cafe, we could see the mist-shrouded pinnacles of Saint Basil's and the Red Star atop the Kremlin.

Habib always had his morning tea with me. I had carried four cartons of Lipton's Green Label tea and an electric kettle with me from India.

One night when we went to the top floor, we found the cafe closed. We came down hungry and exhausted. I went to sleep.

In the morning, Habib came with apples and a leg of roast

chicken. "Enjoy it!" he said, "These are my last night's earnings!" Then he smiled and told me the story.

The previous night, in search of food, he had gone down to the cafe on the lower floor. The shutter opened and a surly fat woman peeped out munching her supper. She growled, "No Food. *Niyet.* Go!"

He returned to his room and was preparing to sleep when he heard a gentle knock at the door. A pause. Again a gentle tap. He opened the door and found the same surly fat woman standing there.

She walked in quickly like a large cat, put her finger across her lips, and bolted the door from inside. For a moment she listened for some sound, and then smiled. Her gold-capped front teeth shone in the dark. Shuddering with delight, she moved towards Habib and took out some roast chicken, apples and rye bread from her basket and uncorked a bottle of wine.

After feeding him luxuriously, she lay naked in his bed and made love to him all night, smothering him under her large cushiony breasts. She smelled of garlic and vodka. At four o'clock in the morning she got up and disappeared, leaving behind the heavy sour smell of her body.

Like the hero of Chekhov's *Don Juan in Russian Style*, Habib had become a target of women's love and was on the verge of collapse. He did not know what to do with this she-demon who came to his bed every night slobbering all over him.

Rejecting Svetlana, he was condemned to sleep with this ogress!

I checked in my luggage and cleared my papers at the counter in the hotel lounge before leaving for the airport.

A dour-faced American, his peaky cap adorned with stars and stripes, was hotly arguing with his interpreter who was asking him to get into the bus for the airport.

The American folded his arms across his chest. "When does the plane leave?"

"At four."

"It's only eleven o'clock now. Why must we go so soon?"

"This bus is leaving. You must get in."

"What the hell! You want me to be sitting on my ass for six hours waiting for your damn plane to take off?"

"But you have to go!"

"Why?"

"That's our system."

"What system? I'll break your fucking system!" he said, and wandered out to have a look at Saint Basil's. The interpretor stood chewing her nails, I thought this American would be arrested.

Finally, the interpreter went to the reception desk and discussed the matter. We boarded the bus and it left without the American. While we sat waiting at the airport until three in the afternoon, a black taxi arrived with the American who joined us, grinning. We spent another six hours in the waiting room. It started snowing. We were asked to relax, have hot borsht, dance and enjoy music.

Bored and yawning, I dozed off in my plastic chair, faintly listening to the dance music wafting in from a nearby room where people were shuffling their feet to rhythm. The dull musical murmurs faded, and I slept heavily.

Suddenly I woke up and blinked my eyes in the cold neon light. I saw an extremely beautiful woman in a Tadjik cap, her black tresses streaming out. I became fully awake in the glare of this refulgent beauty. I can feel a beautiful woman's presence even in darkness. Like the presence of evil. Both charge and ripple the atmosphere with magnetic rays.

I looked at this woman. The sound of music became clearer. Its rhythms stirred my mind. On a wild impulse, I walked over to her and asked her to dance with me.

She smiled and agreed. I led her to a large cement-floored room where people were waltzing to a raucous live band.

She gazed at me. *"Rooski zanaish?* (You know Russian?)"

"Mala...mala...plokha... (Little...little...bad...)"

Using my thirty-word Russian vocabulary, I asked her, *"Kak zavoot* (Your name)?"

"Laila."

"Rooski?"

"Niyet"

"Tadjik?"

"Niyet"

"Kuda?"

"Arab."

"Kuda?"

"Iraq."

She did not know a single word of English. Only Russian and Arabic.

"Indiski?" she asked me.

"Da...da... (Yes...yes...)"

I dug out the Arabic words a maulvi had taught me in school. Not able to construct a full sentence, I spoke with heightened gestures, mixing in a few words of Persian.

"Ya aashiq, tee mashooq (I lover, you beloved)," I said. She looked at me in surprise.

I went on. *"Tee zaalim, ya mazloom* (You cruel, I victim)... *Tee arsh, ya farsh* (You sky, I earth)... *Tee hakim, ya mahkoom* (You ruler, I servant)...*Tee jaabar, ya majboor* (You invader, I helpless)..."

My Arabic speech melted the heart of this Iraqi beauty. She was what I had read about in *The Arabian Nights*. When I ran out of words, I suddenly remembered the geography lessons of my school days, where I had learnt the names of the oceans.

"*Tee Bahr-ul-munjamid*, ya Bahr-e-Oqianoos (You Arctic Ocean, I Atlantic Ocean)," I declared.

She burst into laughter, held and kissed me. "*Tee gavarish Arabski atlichna* (You speak very good Arabic)!"

As I swung her for another round of the waltz, the only dance step I knew, a harsh bell rang and the music stopped. Some one shouted, "The plane is ready to take off ! Board the plane for London!"

I parted from this siren, "We meet again?"

"*Inshallah!*" she said, "*Alvida!*"

I walked to the plane in the falling snow, warmed by thoughts of this unusual beauty.

After a gap of 15 years, I visited Moscow again in 1974 for three weeks. This time the Government of India had sponsored me as an important theatre personality.

The Ministry of Culture gave me a silver passport, a kind of diplomatic privilege to visit the Soviet Union for three weeks.

The Soviet Ambassador invited me to his residence for a small ceremony. We clinked tiny crystal glasses and gulped the vodka. A burning sensation raced down my gullet. I quickly munched a black caviar sandwich.

The ambassador explained the aesthetics of vodka. "It must be finished in one go, followed by a bite of a sandwich.

We Russians love vodka. We call it 'a little sunshine in the stomach.'"

He talked about the new productions of Moscow Art Theatre, and Maly and Vakhtangov, and gave me the names of his favourite actors. With a warm hand-shake he said, "Enjoy your visit to the Soviet Union."

It was snowing when the roaring jet landed at Moskva airport. A dreary Russian winter. The landscape was covered with snow. I emerged from the plane, stepped down the ladder and walked to the hallway. Snow crunched under my feet and became silver mud.

I entered a centrally heated hall, and filed past the customs. A ruddy faced officer went through my passport slowly turning its pages, gazing at each letter. Then pointing to a bench he said in a harsh tone, "Wait there!"

I sat on the bench and watched passengers trickling out. Finally everyone was gone. The waiting room was barren. I stood up and went to the counter window. The officer glared, *"Niyet. Tuda."* He pointed to the bench and locked the barrier.

With heavy steps I walked back to the bench. Fear gripped me. Why had I been held back?

Sitting on the grey-green iron bench I looked through the foggy window glass panes, wondering what had happened. Had they blacklisted me? Was I a *persona non grata*? I started thinking of the crimes I might have committed, even in my dreams ... I might have said something nasty about the Soviet system ... some remark in an off-guard moment ... might have said that the Kremlin is beautiful, gorgeous, supreme, but that there is a rusty rotten nail on the front gate. The party logic: "You Mr. Gargi! Could you find only a rusty rotten nail in the Kremlin? Your eyes fell only on an ugly spot of the great Soviet land? You are maligning the socialist order ... the system ... you are helping the capitalist world ... the enemy ... you are ..."

I must have spoken something against Russia ... must have uttered some foul word ... Maybe someone had reported me ... I had married an American blonde and gone to the States to teach Indian drama in Seattle ... had been awarded a special achievement award ... a capitalist bribe! ... I delved into my soul ... into my dreams ... my nightmares ... and worked out my punishment ... Siberia ... or a bullet ...

I was startled by the heavy stamping of boots ... twelve Russian soldiers in knee-high black boots goose-stepped past, guns in hand ... marching ... tight-lipped, tight-chinned ... waiting for a command. Looking at me, they stomped away and disappeared into the control room.

Suddenly I saw a Russian girl bent over the railing, her silken hair streaming out of her fur cap. She held a bunch of white flowers and was hotly arguing with the officer.

I sat frozen on the bench, not daring to move or twitch a muscle. Finally, the officer motioned to me with a flick of his hand. I walked over to him.

The girl told me that there had been some mistake in my passport. The visa stamp was valid for entry between 9th November and 9th December. I had landed one day late. No one had checked the dates. An Indian cannot decipher Russian letters. November and December appear the same. The girl gave me forty roubles for tea and food, took my passport, and rushed to the Ministry of Culture to renew the visa.

I went back to my bench. An aggressive and powerful-looking woman in police uniform, a revolver strapped to her belt, appeared. She was at least six feet tall. This amazon ordered me in English to carry my suitcase and I walked with her to the general ward.

I picked up the heavy suitcase, lugged it through a little

iron gate which the amazon locked behind me, and was led in to a large hall. I sat on an iron bench. She left.

I waited for two hours. Nobody in sight. The sky became dark and heavy.

The amazon reappeared and said, "It's too late. The girl won't come. You'd better stay in our hotel nearby. Pick up your luggage."

I followed her, frozen to my bones as gusts of arctic wind slapped me ... a Siberian prisoner. We arrived at a dark little two-storey hotel.

She took out an ancient key, one of those gigantic keys which I had seen in Gogol's period plays, and opened a heavy creaking wooden door. A whiff of damp, stale air hit me. Going up the dingy staircase, she fixed a large key in a thick door, clanked it open and ushered me into a low-ceilinged foyer. Closing the door, she said to me, "That's your room. Your bed. I'll see you tomorrow."

Two chubby blondes with red cheeks, pearl blue eyes and silken pigtails sat at the telephone desk. They appeared to be of peasant stock.

I put my luggage in a tiny room. A small double-barred window opened outside. I came out of the room to breathe, and tried to talk to the girls, but they did not know a single word of any other language except Russian. My Russian vocabulary made the girls giggle. Finally, I said, *"Ya lublu Moskva* ... (I love Moscow). *Ya lublu vas* (I love you)." The girls burst into laughter.

I wanted to use the telephone. Both frowned, *"Niyet".* I paced up and down the little corridor aching to go out and breathe fresh air, but could not find the door. "Please open it," I asked these girls. Again they laughed, *"Kluch, niyet,"* they gestured with their hands. The key had been taken away by the amazon.

I was locked in. I gasped. How to get out of this hell-hole? I started beating the walls. I heard a child cry. A young man with a clipped black moustache appeared from another room. He looked me over from head to foot and asked "Are you a fresh arrival?"

"Yes"

"Staying in this hotel?"

"Yes."

He gave a dry laugh, "It's not a hotel. It's a prison. I was brought here seven days ago with my wife and child and told that I should stay in this hotel to catch my connecting flight to Teheran. I'm a rug dealer. I boarded a plane for London and was to change to Aeroflot because it's cheaper. But they tell me that there is no seat in the plane. Every day it is the same story. I've to buy food and milk for my child and spend in pounds. The rate of exchange is shocking. One pound to two rubles. A cup of milk and a sandwich cost me a fortune. My wife weeps. My child cries. I'm in misery. I don't know how to get out."

Fear paralysed me. Everything was unreachable. I could not contact the Indian Embassy nor any writer friend. Not the Gypsy Theatre director Barkan, nor my translator Smirnoff.

That night, I had horrible dreams.

I woke up with a splitting headache.

Pale sunlight fell on me, cold and sickly. I looked through the window and saw a dull yellow sun in the foggy sky. Far away, blank white spaces ...

Somebody knocked on my door. I opened it and saw the amazon in full uniform, the revolver in her waist belt, and the same Gogolian key. Smiling broadly, she said, "Welcome to the Soviet Union! You are our guest of honour!" and presented me with a bouquet of roses. I took the roses in utter bewilderment.

Was it a joke or a dream?

She beamed. "Your visa has come. Your escort is waiting outside. Please come with me. We are honoured by your visit."

As I reached out to pick up my suitcase, she barred my way, "Let me help you." She carried it like a trophy through the dingy foyer down the damp steps. I felt the winds of freedom.

A black car with the Hammer and Sickle flag and the girl with flowers were waiting for me.

5

I was combing Europe, devouring its cities and arts, discovering new faces, new ideas, and new friends. Joining a delegation of young writers, painters and poets from Europe, I went to Warsaw for the Youth Festival. A clutch of Polish blondes greeted us at the railway station, blowing kisses. Sakshi had also come to the Festival as a member of the Indian delegation. Many fat wives of industrialists, by paying the full fare and a donation, had joined the gaggle. But the organisers needed glamour. Sakshi supplied it.

We were entertained for twelve days with free food, dances and cultural programmes. The Polish cooks had been warned that Hindus do not eat beef because they worship the cow as a mother. Since the meat had to be of a different variety, the waitresses served curried veal. While the Indians were licking their yellowed fingers, enjoying each morsel, someone told them that they were eating the flesh of a tender calf ... son of the holy cow. They ran out to vomit and purify their mouths. But some found the veal delicious, and told the waitresses not to leak out the secret!

I was charmed by the genius of Polish designers. Above all by their women. Walking down the main street I would stare at them in their exquisite caps, coats, pullovers and skirts. I wondered why Moscow women were stodgy, whereas the Poles were dressed in high fashion.

An actress explained. "Poland is poor, and poverty has sharpened our artistic sense. We use rags of different textures, colours and strips to create our own designs. Look? the sleeves of my coat are from a discarded piece of velvet, its collar is of fox skin, and the pockets are cut out of an old blanket. Every Polish woman is wearing a personal design."

At night there was a banquet. Pablo Neruda, the Cuban poet Nicholas Guillen, the German poet Steffan Hermeline, Lenin Prize winner Anna Seghers, Mulk Raj Anand, I, and some painters and actresses were present. Sakshi too was at the party.

We clinked our glasses and toasted world peace. Dinner, cognac, cigars, and the Blue Danube. Everyone danced. Mulk was waltzing with a Polish actress.

Guillen walked up to Sakshi and addressed her loudly in Spanish, praising her beauty. She looked at him blankly.

He asked her to dance, and put his hand on her shoulder.

"Remove your paw!" she snapped.

We all persuaded her to dance with Guillen, but she refused.

"Why won't you dance with him ?" Neruda pleaded.

"Not with this baboon!"

"A great poet is begging you. The greatest amongst us. Dance with him."

"I don't care if he is the king of England ! He stinks."

Guillen did not understand what was happening.

Turning to him, Neruda explained in Spanish, "She is afraid of her husband."

"Five thousand miles away in India? Nonsense!" Guillen grinned and extended his hand.

"Get away from me !"

Guillen had a swarthy complexion, broad nostrils, and thick chocolate lips. He was a Cuban mulatto with animality and passion in his eyes. He could not stand his rejection. A savage anger welled up in him and crimson streaks shot from his eyes. Grabbing Sakshi, he started dragging her to the dance floor, yelling in Spanish. She shrieked. The waitresses ran to her help, and with great difficulty we managed to extricate her from his hairy grip.

The following day Guillen purchased a book — *English-Spanish-English*— practised all day, and learnt twenty of the choicest sentences. He appeared at dinner, presented a bouquet to Sakshi and said, "I luv you ... beaoothiful ... your eyes ... senorita ... I luv you ..."

Going down on his knees, he started to recite a love poem in Spanish which he had composed celebrating her beauty. I watched him serenading her, his hand on his heart, his mouth pouring out honey and roses.

Neruda said to Sakshi, "It's beautiful in Spanish. It moves me to tears. You don't understand him. Without his language, he is just a dumb beast."

Moving on, I reached Berlin for a five-day halt. I did not like the German language with its gutteral sounds of 'ukh', 'ikh', 'und', 'kind', etc. My distaste for the language had been aggravated after I saw Charlie Chaplin's *The Great Dictator* in which he barks out a nonsensical German speech in a high-pitched, raucous voice.

My host asked me if I would like to see a Brecht play. *Mother Courage* was playing. I had not heard of Brecht as a playwright, but had read a poem or two by him which had not made any impression on me.

That evening I went to see *Mother Courage* with my interpreter Kitty Schmitz, a buxom girl with reddish hair. We hurried through the gate, the outer gallery and lobby, and entered the crowded hall as the lights were being dimmed. I groped for my seat. Kitty sat next to me. The chalk-white safety curtain painted with the "Picasso Dove" went up.

On the revolving stage, two young men yoked to a wagon walk with heavy steps. Mother Courage (Helene Weigel) in a full-length skirt and padded grey jacket, a pewter spoon tucked in her pocket, stands in the wagon singing a marching song in her bugle-like voice. Her dumb daughter (Angelica Hurwicz) sits by her side playing a harmonica. The wagon rumbles along. Two soldiers stop the wagon and order Mother to show her papers. She whips out a knife. A scuffle. The soldiers drag away one of her sons for conscription.

Some scenes still stand out in my memory : Mother flirts with the soldiers to hide her identity, refusing to recognise the body of her son. As the soldiers bend forward to examine the face of her son, Mother lets out a silent cry, a dumb wail. This 'silent cry' became the world-known cry of a mother's anguish. In another scene, the dumb daughter detects an enemy attack on the village. She goes up to the roof of her house and starts beating a drum to awaken the sleeping village. The enemy soldiers fix their rifles on X-shaped wooden stands and yell at her to stop, but she goes on beating the drum louder and louder. Finally, as the soldiers shoot her down, she gives a last beat with her limp hand and collapses.

In the end, Mother loses everything—two sons, a daughter, and all her possessions. She ties a rope around her waist and drags the wagon across the battlefield, staggering in a whorl of darkness. Mother—dehumanised, stubborn, mean, foolish, a beast—learns nothing from experience.

She reminded me of my own mother.

When the play was over, I continued to sit in my chair, overpowered by emotion. Kitty tapped my shoulder, "Get up, it's over."

We came out of the theatre and crossed the oily Spree river, walked down Frederichstrasse, turned left and reached my hotel, where Kitty asked me to wait in the foyer. She returned half an hour later with the German text of *Mother Courage,* a package of cheese, sausages, and a bottle of wine. On the way up to my room, the elevator man—an old soldier—glared at us suspiciously.

Entering my room, Kitty cast a look around, switched on the table lamp and sat down in a chair. With German efficiency, she uncorked the bottle, poured some wine in two glasses, and we drank to each other's health. Munching cheese, she started translating the songs of Brecht's play to me. I wrote the words down in a notebook, comparing the translation with the one by Eric Bentley. We continued working till midnight.

I heard footsteps coming down the corridor. I was afraid to have Kitty in my room that late. "Don't worry", she said. "I've bribed that old rascal with ten West German marks and sealed his mug. Nobody will come up."

Closing the book, she switched off the light. In the soft glow of the city lights filtering through the glass windows I saw Kitty in a golden silhouette as she peeled off her clothes. Soon we were in bed. I felt her long arms, mouth, neck and moist breasts and hips, smooth and shiny like oiled mirrors ... her breath covering me with sweet warmth as we dissolved into each other.

"*Ich liebe du*", she babbled in German. Putting her finger to my lips, she hissed, "Sssssshh! *ich liebe du* ...!" Prattling and babbling, her gibberish assumed an occult power, transmitting sensations ... moons circling in our flesh ... binding us in a hallucinatory relationship. In her tight embrace, I felt something pricking my chest. It was a gold cross she was wearing on a chain around her neck.

She woke up early the next morning. As she bent over me to say good morning, I saw the deep impress of the cross on her breast.

I stayed on in Berlin for one month, watching plays and attending Brecht's rehearsals.

Every night I would return to my hotel, located near a high barbed-wire wall guarded by soldiers. As I walked under the elms on the deserted boulevard towards my hotel, I would pass the skeletons of a block of bombed-out buildings with their curved beams and hollow ruins. These were Hitler's bunkers, and he had died in one of these underground cellars.

I always shrank with fear whenever I walked past these bunkers— still alive, dangerous, breathing horror. They had a strange pull. I was sure that if I went too close they would suck me in. They had a sinister attraction. The wind moaned through them, fear still pulsating and breathing through their lungs.

Kitty often took me to the West Berlin section in the Underground. Though the two Berlins were divided crazily, a common network of rails ran under the streets. As the train rumbled through the tunnel, its lights would suddenly blink off, a sign that we had changed territories from poorly-lit, dreary stalls to brightly lit stations—well stocked, rich and flashy.

I spent an evening with Brecht in his apartment. His room smelled of coffee and leather: leather-lined chairs, leather-bound books, a leather jacket, a leather cap. A fat cigar in his mouth exuded pungent fumes. He was suffering from heart trouble and avoided meeting strangers. But perhaps my being an Indian, one who had patiently watched him rehearsing, had made it possible for me to reach him.

He poured some thick black German coffee in two cups, and offered me one. I took a sip and looked around the austere room, at his pursed lips gripping the cigar, and wondered how to break the silence. I asked him whether he had ever been to India.

He smiled. "No, and I don't think I will. I have travelled enough. I don't want to move out of Berlin now. I have a lot of work to finish, and I am bound to my theatre and my players. Good actors are rare. Most of my actors are familiar with my style and thinking, and it is comfortable to work with them."

He took another puff of his cigar. Silence. No movement in the room except the slow circling smoke of his cigar.

"I have read *Mother Courage* in translation," I said.

"My interpreter tells me that it does not do full justice to the original."

He grimaced. "The English language is weak, like their tea. It cannot carry the thick power and many-layered texture of German speech. Eric Bentley has used the phrase 'alienation' to describe my dramatic process of *verfremdun*. It's an incorrect translation. My characters are objectified to the viewer, not alienated from them. The audience must be hypnotised by action, word, colour and emotion, and then shocked out of it. Emotion is very important... I want my audience to sit back after their involvement and reflect...see the historical process through reason. Look at the Kabuki actor. He delivers his lines with all the intensity, emotion and concentration he can muster, and yet remains aloof from the audience."

Like the Kabuki performer Brecht's actors were charged with gut feeling. They would set the audience on emotional fire, then douse them with cold water of logic, using direct comments, songs and masks.

I had met some of his actors and actresses sitting casually in the little coffee room attached to the theatre. The tables were rubbed smooth from use and the benches were greasy. Coffee was set out in large metal drums for the actors to help themselves to. I saw no beautiful actors or actresses in the entire ensemble. There was Helene Weigel, who would sit on her haunches and smoke cigarettes like a gypsy woman, and Angelica Hurwicz who was plump and wore thick glasses. They looked like charwomen.

I had heard that Brecht did not like beautiful women. I wondered if this was true, as he had numerous affairs. Now sitting with him, I ventured to ask, "I hear that you don't like beautiful women?"

"Beautiful women distract" he smiled. "They are good for bed, not for the stage. Fools marry beautiful women, and spend their lives promoting them. Marry a talented actress, and let her express your soul on stage."

He himself had married Helene Weigel, a leathery-faced woman who had no sex appeal, but had immortalized the role of Mother Courage.

Brecht was meticulous in choice of actors and artists. He assembled top designers, composers and performers around him. Costumes of the working class were treated by specialists to look worn and overused. Actors, once trained, were reluctant to leave him. I watched rehearsals of *The Caucasian Chalk Circle,* and was overpowered by its mathematical precision, geometrical groupings, and the beautifully worked-out half-masks which were almost a part of the facial make-up, heightening dramatic effect. Many years later, in 1966, I happened to see *Chalk Circle* in New York in a production directed by Herbert Blau at the Lincoln Centre. I was appalled by the heavily-carved, abnormally clumsy masks he had used, which not only hid the faces of the performers, but destroyed all emotion.

In London I camped for some months with my cousin Bhagwan Garga, who had come here to become a film director, but was now selling Swiss watches in a shop at Tottenham Court Road. He used to get up at seven, make a quick cup of coffee, munch a croissant, grab his umbrella and run in the freezing cold to catch the tube. He would return late in the evening, drained, earning six pounds a week.

I decided not to take up a job. I wrote articles on Indian

theatre and dance and sent these to Russian, German, Polish and French papers with flashy photographs I had brought with me from India. They published the articles and paid me well. This was supplemented with occasional talks on the BBC.

I would sleep till nine, make coffee, read the newspapers and go out at eleven to wander the streets—Piccadilly, Leicester Square, Oxford Street, dipping into their bookshops, art galleries and little cafes. In the evening, I would see a play or a friend, or walk two miles to El Cubano, a Cuban restaurant at Knightsbridge where orange-eyed black waitresses with large shiny earrings served spicy foaming coffee for one shilling a cup.

These were the days when Genet, Beckett and Osborne were being discovered and staged, and Peter Hall, Peter Brook and Kenneth Tynan had stunned London with their theatrical brilliance.

In my wild adventures I met Joan Rodkar, a Jewish TV producer and actress, who took me under her wing. With her I went to various parties.

Doris Lessing's was an open house for me, and I would often be at her dinner parties. She had surrendered her Party card and was critical of the economic and literary values of Moscow. At her get-togethers, ideological discussions lasted till the small hours of the morning. Parts of these discussions appeared in *The Golden Notebook*. I could recognise the faces of some of her friends, specially those of Joan Rodkar and the Polish ideologue John Cotts.

Sometimes I would go to Doris early in the evening and find her by the stove-side reading, scribbling or correcting proofs. She loved cooking. Metal pots full of thick meat gravy simmered and filled her room with the aroma. Occasionally she would sip a spoonful of the curry to test its consistency.

Doris had short black hair, luminous skin and sparkling eyes. When she smiled, her cheeks dimpled. In temperament she was more Mediterranean than British. She spilled her charm, doling out sensual warmth to people engaged in literary discussions in her apartment. Her eleven-year-old son always watched her suspiciously, guarding her lest his beautiful mother fall for some man.

One night I was the last to leave her apartment. She came down the stairs to see me off and gave me a goodnight kiss. Feeling the warmth of her ample bosom and her breath of apples and cognac, I held her and tried to kiss her, but she pushed me away. "You're too late, Balwant. I already have a lover!"

I walked home wondering what she thought of me. A boor, a sex-hungry Indian?

The next evening she was the same vivacious Doris. She hugged me with the same warmth.

"Have you read anything by me?" she asked me one day.

I told her I hadn't, so she took out a paperback edition of her novel *The Grass is Singing,* and gave it to me.

The action of the novel is set in Rhodesia, and is about the sexual relationship of a native negro boy and a white woman, the seduction and excitement of the colour mix, details of flesh, body, mind, racial hatred and attraction ... also descriptions of social and political cross-currents. In life, her dimpled laughter and bohemian attitude appeared innocent, but these hid a deep knowledge of human behaviour. It frightened and attracted me.

I was living at Cromwell Road, parallel to Hyde Park. London had not yet switched to central heating, and the houses were cold at night. I would shiver in my bed. Even though I fed the gas heater shillings, the moment the meter would stop ticking, the room became ice cold. I was sure that one morning I would be found frozen. I wondered why the English people, masters of the largest empire in the world, should be fifty years behind France. Perhaps the British love misery. They love the fog, cold, rain and sleet, and are always carrying an umbrella in the crook of their arm.

One day, Doris said, "You are not used to this cold. You can sleep in my bed. I am going to Africa for some time." She gave me the keys of her apartment. An electric heater hung on the wall, sending out its rays. I slept cosily in her bed, blessing her.

I moved in theatre circles and met the amazingly knowledgeable Tana Sayers, an Italian-born American intellectual, a guru in the visual and dramatic arts, and a friend of Joan and Doris. She educated me in contemporary theatrical aesthetics. I would see a play every week with Tana or Joan or Doris, and go for late night coffee with them, soaking up new trends in the arts. My education was verbal, based on personal contact, watching things happening on the spot.

I saw many first-run plays which later became classics. Particularly baffling was Peter Hall's production of Beckett's *Waiting for Godot*. Nobody seemed to understand the play, yet the hall was full of inquisitive spectators lured to the theatre by the rave reviews. I saw the play and could not make head or tail of it. A woman who had been working as an usher in the theatre for the past twelve years was quoted by a daily paper as saying that she had "never seen such a senseless and idiotic play in her life." But the theatricality of the play—its irrelevant dialogues with philosophical and startling absurdity—drew crowds.

In one party I met Kenneth Tynan, who at the young age of twenty-seven had become the drama critic of *The Observer*, and was a sensation in the theatre circles. His brilliantly penetrating reviews lashed out at stodgy British productions and changed the face of London theatre. He was tall, with a pale oval face, and wore a long tweed coat with leather buttons. He stammered as he uttered his dazzling words. One evening Kenneth and I went to see Giraudoux's *Tiger at the Gates*, in which Michael Redgrave played Hector. After the show we went to a small Indian restaurant for dinner.

Mopping up curry with a piece of chappatti, he said, "Indian curry is like shit. A greenish yellow shit. But I love it."

Changing tracks, he talked about his plans to make a film on *Macbeth*. So far the three witches had been portrayed mostly as old hags with hooked noses and ragged skirts. Kenneth wanted to cast three nude blondes as sexy witches who would fog Macbeth's mind.

"Beauty is frightening," he said. "It creates hallucination and strikes terror. The West does not know it, but the Japanese do. Their witches and evil spirits are beautiful. Like cherry blossoms, they evoke the idea of death. Of murder and doom. Three nude blondes will be my witches."

Years later, he did fulfil his dream when he switched from his revolutionary leftism to pornographic art (and produced the shockingly lewd *Oh Calcutta!*). He filmed *Macbeth* with three nude witches, shot in a foggy Scottish winter amidst castles, turrets and ancient heaths. The actresses, shivering in the icy winds, covered themselves with thermal blankets and stripped only during shots.

The Chinese Writers Union invited me to be their guest for a month. From London, in one giant leap forward over two continents, I arrived in Peking and stayed in a newly built hotel with marble pillars.

The next morning I was awakened by quaint, high-pitched caterwauls. I peeped out of my fifth-floor window and saw an army of waiters, cooks and butlers—the entire hotel staff— in shorts and white shirts, doing their morning drill. A chubby young woman in pigtails and a military cap was giving commands. A compulsory warm-up. It was inspiring to watch this early morning ritual which was a prelude to their work .

My hosts offered to show me the Great Wall of China, the Yangtze River and Shanghai, but I preferred to stay in Peking. When I visit a country I do not want to 'pocket' cities and monuments. I am happy with one painting in my room. I want to savour it, live with it. So also with cities and friends.

This was during the Cultural Revolution, when Mao raised the slogan 'Let a thousand flowers bloom!' Writers, painters and intellectuals had been promised freedom of expression, but when they voiced their secret thoughts they were arrested and imprisoned. They became their own spies.

I phoned Siao Emi and Mao Tung whom I had met in Moscow, but they were always busy in meetings. Siao's wife, a German Jewish beauty who had fallen in love with him during the World War and had settled in Peking, paid occasional visits to Berlin. The German language and music pulled her back. I had met her in 1955 at the Berliner Ensemble where she was taking photographs of Brecht's production of *The Caucasian Chalk Circle*. She had asked me to call on her if I ever visited Peking and had given me her card. I could not reach any one of them.

I enjoyed roaming the streets, through dingy old shops filled with curios and folk crafts. The Chinese are born with a brush in their hand. Their calligraphy is a work of art, a painting of flowing rhythms. Even their chopsticks have always been an enigma to me. How they pick each grain of rice from a bowl and toss it into the mouth. Their fingers are almost electronic.

I went to see the Summer Palace and the Lake which the Dowager Empress Tzu'hsi had built at the end of the last century. She would sit behind a latticed window every evening and watch handsome youths diving in the lake. The most handsome was chosen to spend a night in bed with her. In the morning the royal executioners chopped off his head to shut his mouth for ever.

I spent time attending Peking Opera performances and rehearsals—actors doing elaborate make-up in wild and strong colours, watching the transformation of a beardless smooth-skinned actor—almost a woman—into a ferocious warrior. I saw Mei Lan-feng in the role of the beautiful daughter of a general. Unbelievable grace at the age of sixty-five. But it did not surprise me. I had seen India's Kathak dancers past seventy acting as bewitching females, teaching courtesans the art of coquetry.

A day with the ninety-four-year old Zen painter Chi Pai-shea was rewarding. I purchased an original Chi "frog" from his curio shop. All his life Chi had been painting frogs, crabs, shrimps, and squirrels. Loaded with black paint, his brush would draw a squirrel in one stroke—its furry dark bushy tail quivering, almost alive.

Most memorable was the Peking Duck, a four-hundred-year-old restaurant. The hotel manager guided me there by drawing a map, and told me that the restaurant had been named after the famous Peking duck.

I went into the main bazaar looking at each shop. After thirty shops I asked where the Peking Duck was. A man told me that I had left it behind. I walked back, reading the hieroglyphic characters. Again I missed it. I retraced my steps, minutely examining the shops, I saw a very narrow lane, a slit in the busy street. I entered it and found the restaurant.

The smell of soya sauce and steaming Chinese flavours came in puffs. Live lobsters shrieked as they sizzled over flaming ovens. The smell of roasted duck and sea fish floated in the air. I inhaled this cocktail of flavours.

The Peking duck is treated like a concubine. It is kept in a water pond and fed special worms. The duck lazes and fattens. Then it is taken out. A ritual follows: the feathers are plucked, and it is cleaned and stuffed. After it is baked, it is brought to the table, steaming and crusted. A master chef wields his long knife with the precision of a surgeon, carving the duck with utmost delicacy lest it be 'injured'.

I ordered a piece of this royal duck. Each delicious bite melted in my mouth.

Eating in China, like India, is not a social activity. It is a very personal act. The entire body is tasting food, juices flowing and dissolving. When a father and his sons eat in a joint family, they do not talk. Each one concentrates on his food. There is complete silence, except for the sound of chopsticks and slurps.

Looking up between bites, my eyes caught Pablo Neruda sitting with a woman, absorbed in conversation. When he picked up pieces of the sliced duck, he ate them with the same intensity with which he was conversing. I wondered who the woman was. She was sensual, Spanish-looking. A friend, a writer, a peace-worker? Perhaps Neruda had divorced his first wife. My curiosity grew.

I got up and walked over to him. I stood near the table, but they both continued talking. Neruda did not raise his eyes.

"Hello !" I said

He looked up and gave me a puzzled glance.

"Please don't disturb us now. Can't you see that I am

with my wife?."

I walked back to my table. So it was his new wife. I had visualised this event seven years ago, and wanted to confirm my prophecy.

Some months later I learnt that Neruda had left Delia del Carril, his wife, after eighteen years of comradeship. She had lived with him through his days of exile, through war, destruction, and danger, carrying revolutionary messages through Spain, South America and Europe. He had called her "a thread of steel and honey", but had snapped this thread without Delia's knowledge. He wrote a book of love poems in praise of this new woman, Matilde Urrutia, a lush copper-haired female of great passion. He did not put his name on the book lest it hurt Delia, but she recognised the style, as did many of Neruda's friends. It hurt her the most—almost killed her. Neruda was not only a faithless lover, but a sneak with no guts to face her, a crumbling skeleton. I felt guilty. I should not have wished Neruda to get rid of her when they had visited my house in Delhi.

On my way back from Peking I stopped at Ulan Bator, the capital of Outer Mongolia, named after their revolutionary hero. A slim pock-marked Party teacher was my guide.

He drove me to a far-off farm which had only an imaginary boundary. Three Mongolian women on horseback came galloping towards us, hooves emitting sparks. They asked me to ride with them, but I was afraid lest I fall off and break my bones. But they insisted, literally lifting me onto a horse without a saddle or bridle. As the horse shot off, I grabbed its flying red mane and shrieked. One of the women overtook me and stopped the horse, and I dismounted.

I supped with them and drank mare's milk in a large silver bowl. It tasted like sour whey, and I could not bear more than one sip. The woman said, "Drink it. It'll make you strong like a horse. In India you drink cow's milk and you become a cow!"

My guide stuffed me with the history of Mongolia and their legendary hero Genghis Khan, giving graphic descriptions of his glorious deeds. His picture—a slit-eyed broad-boned Khan, with a thin feathery white beard—was up in every Mongolian home.

I marvelled at the power of Genghis Khan, the greatest conquerer in world history, who built an empire from a nomad's village. His horses drank the water of the Pacific Ocean on one side and of the Danube on the other. He waged fifty-two battles in his life, his army always one-third that of the enemy's, and he conquered wherever he set foot. He united the East and the West, opened trade routes and diplomatic missions, and gave a special place to philosophers and architects in his court.

In Mongolia, land is not a commodity. It is God's gift. You can pitch your tent anywhere even today. Its area is half that of India, and its population only two million. In this vast space, swept by Arctic winds, where the noon sun shivers and sends cold rays, you don't see a human being for miles. I felt the beauty and magic of unending space. Three days in Mongolia were like three years. Time stretched like its landscape.

My guide, who seldom shared his secret thoughts with anyone, became my friend. I was a complete foreigner, who might never come back to this harsh land. One day he said, "Russia is robbing us. We are a rich country. We have seven million horses—three horses per head. And sheep, wool, furs and gold. Russia is buying our ermine and sable at the lowest rate and selling it to the western world at high prices. Why? A brother should not rob a brother."

He turned, looked back carefully and resumed, "You know, after the First World War, Mongolia was carved into two halves. One was grabbed by the Chinese and the other by the Russians. Why don't they let us become one?"

He took me to a country fair where women were selling embroidered fur jackets, coats, beads, metal jars, and leatherware. I was attracted by a skinned lynx, its rippling greyish-brown fur streaked with white. He presented it to me as a gift from Mongolia.

That night as I slept in my hotel room at the end of the corridor, I felt a mysterious presence. I looked around in the dark. Two greenish-yellow eyes glittered ... a furry body slithered and heaved. I immediately put on the light. It was the lynx.

I lifted the skin, stuffed it in my suitcase, placed it in the bathroom and locked the door.

I returned to India after three years.

During my absence a local apothecary had moved into my house with a distant friend of a friend of mine to whom I had given the house keys. When I entered the courtyard I saw that two brown yellow pits had been dug in my courtyard. They looked like two gouged eyes staring at me.

The apothecary had been pounding herbs and spices in these pits. The smell of pungent fumes hung in the air. He had arranged all my books and papers carefully and stored these in a large wicker box. When I opened the box, a dank smell hit me.

White ants had eaten away my revolutionary notes, articles, rough sketches, photographs and negatives.

I emptied the box into a garbage dump.

6

My house was always open in my absence. Friends came, camped, rolled their beddings and left, and new visitors crashed on the cotton-stuffed pads. The house was like a commune. Once, a contingent of twenty-three actors, writers and poets—delegates from Punjab on their way to Calcutta for a cultural conference—stayed overnight in my house. Boiled rice and *daal* were the standard menu which my cook prepared in large quantities.

I returned from Bombay late in the evening after an abortive film assignment, and saw some strangers sitting in my room smoking *sulfa*. A flame leapt from the *chillam*, lighting the oily face of a tribal.

Habib Tanvir had brought a troupe of tribal actors from

his native place in Madhya Pradesh. Finding no other place, they were camping in my house. Lalu Ram was their leader—a short-statured, frog-eyed singer-actor. He stood up, folded his hands, bent over double and said that they were grateful for the hospitality.

Habib was rehearsing *Mrichchakatika* (The Little Clay Cart) which Begum Qudsia Zaidi had translated into Hindi as *Mitti ki Gaadi*. Songs were composed in my little den by Niaz Haider, a crazy alcoholic poet steeped in Urdu classics and Hindi folk traditions.

Begum Zaidi, founder-President of the Hindustani Theatre, was one of the most beautiful and artistic women Delhi has ever known. She smoked an expensive hookah with a silver-wired *chillam* and a winding silver-tipped pipe, and chewed betel-leaves of the choicest variety out of a filigreed box which her page carried around. Her knowledge of the arts, period literature and language was amazing. She had a passion for presenting Indian classical plays in modern idiom and would translate and adapt plays into Urdu with great speed and versatility. Sometimes after rehearsals, she would come to my house with Habib and the players and drink tea in my courtyard, discussing details of the production.

Pulling at the silver stem of her hookah she would say "I'll build the best theatre in Delhi ... productions of Brecht ... Shaw ... Kalidasa ... Shudraka ... Agha Hashr Kashmiri. Just now there are only trashy plays ... cheap and crude comedies. I'll teach these *Delhiwallas* what good theatre is, and whip them into shape." She spoke in impeccable, sparkling Urdu. Very few people knew that she was a Punjabi from Amritsar. Her courtly grace and feminine charm mesmerised people. She commanded, and the highest submitted.

She lived in a bungalow in Jamia Milia by the bank of

the Yamuna with a troupe of servants. Her husband was the Vice-Chancellor of Aligarh University, where she would sometimes go for a few days to join him. Her living expenses were high and she did not know how to economise.

"Why do you need seven servants?" I suggested. "Cut down their number."

"I can't," she said. "All of them are essential. The cook. Old butler. Chauffeur. Gardener, Watchman. Errand boy. Mughlani who sews and irons my clothes."

Her aristocratic nature could not bear the thought of dismissing anyone of them.

When *Mitti ki Gaadi* opened at the Fine Arts Theatre, Pandit Nehru came to see the performance. He sat in the third row with the Begum. A few of us sat behind them in the fourth row. When the play stretched beyond three hours, Nehru looked restlessly at his radium watch. Begum Zaidi nudged him, "Wah, Panditji! You are not bored by the long-winded speeches in Parliament? Don't look at your watch. See the play!"

Nehru obeyed.

After the show, Nehru went on stage for a photograph with the actors. Blinking in the strong lights, he shouted, "Qudsia! Come to the stage." She waved her hand and threw a bright smile. "No Panditji, I won't come. You get yourself photographed. Not I." She did not go on stage.

She travelled with the players, giving performances of *Mitti ki Gaadi* and *Shakuntala* under great financial stress because the theatre had eaten up her personal reserves. Travelling in the heat and dust, in a congested third class compartment, her delicate temperament could not bear the strain. While camping in a small town for the night during the tour, she had a heart attack and collapsed before her loving husband could reach her.

I had wished the College Road of Mandi House, dotted with theatres and cultural societies, be renamed Begum Qudsia Zaidi Road. I wrote letters to the Corporation and urged a few important persons to look into the matter. But the Begum was an aristocrat, and belonged to no political party. The cultural nominations were the prerogative of politically-motivated persons.

Qudsia left behind hardly any photographs. But she left a deep imprint on everyone who had ever met her.

7

It was late evening. As the electricity had failed, I lit a candle and sat in the courtyard, trying to read a letter in the flickering flame.

I heard a car stop in the service lane and opened the door.

Amrita Pritam stood there dressed in a raw silk shirt, shalwar and pink *chunni,* her hair falling on her shoulders. I was surprised by her visit so late in the evening.

She walked into the courtyard and extended her hand.

"Good-bye!" she said.

"Why are you wishing me good-bye?" I asked, taken aback.

"Not to you. To this horrible Delhi. I'm leaving for Bombay."

"When?"

"Just now."

Her lover Imroz was outside in the car. I went out and invited him in. He was a slim, shy, golden-coloured youth who made sketches for the Urdu magazine, *Shama*.

He was reluctant to come in. I almost dragged him into the courtyard.

"Why are you going to Bombay?" I asked Amrita.

"There will be nobody to question me—as to whom I live with, why I smoke, why I rebel. I have friends there. I have had enough of Delhi. Let the crumb-seekers live here. God bless them. But I am going."

I seated them in the courtyard and brought out a bottle of Hungarian wine and three glasses. I uncorked the bottle, poured the wine, and we clinked our glasses.

"To love!"

"To happiness!"

"To destiny!"

After the ceremonial drink, we felt free and more animated. The courtyard, the bougainvillea, the champak with its faint fragrance, and the candle light added to our dreamy conversation.

She lit a cigarette and said, "I'm what I am. This 'I' is Amrita Pritam. People want to change it. Hah!" She gave a throaty laugh.

Taking a deep puff of her cigarette, she talked about life, love, dreams. "Many times I have dreamt of an ocean ... high waves ... a beach ... a hut ... a lamp burning. I hear a splash ... I peer out ... someone is tethering his boat ... he walks on the beach and comes to me. His face is covered ... an image haunting me ... I elope with him, breaking my chains ... complete in myself, like an island ..."

She spoke as if in a trance. The thought of eloping with her lover had given her strength. She continued: "I always invoke the tombs to open up and speak. Our people are worse than the dead. There is a conspiracy of silence. Bandits in every street, in every city, in every country ... ready to pounce. No writer speaks. They are dogs tied with a chain. Their poems bark. But I want them to bark with honesty."

Amrita recalled her emotional phase of the fifties. She had loved two men at the same time, and dreamt of both. She wore two wrist watches, gifts from her lovers. ... There was mystery in these watches. When she turned to her first lover, the other watch stopped. When she turned to the second, the first watch stopped. She could communicate with her watches, listen to their ticking in a secret code, and understand the message.

"I am very sentimental", she sighed. "I have celebrated love in my poems. It was unreachable, like the sky. It always eluded me. Then I fell in love with Imroz ..." She looked at him and he lowered his eyes, embarrassed, his lips trembling. "Yes, I fell in love with him ... passionate, satisfying, beautiful ... My love has been a constant struggle, full of tension ... a war of two contradictory emotions ... I am a victim of this Mahabharata within me."

Imroz had sat quietly throughout her conversation. He looked at Amrita with a warm smile, proud of her love, overcome by the feeling that the legendary queen of Punjabi poetry had chosen him. She was leaving for Bombay with him—defying society, heading to danger, in search of happiness.

As she sat there in the darkness, tears welled up in her eyes. "I have to go now."

We hugged each other and I went out to see them off. They sat in their car, a Fiat which they had jointly bought—their first sharing of life's adventures, emotional and financial. He turned the ignition key, put it in gear, and the car raced away. She had set out on a stormy journey.

It was Diwali in 1960. I had gone to Blue Pottery to have lunch with Gurcharan Singh, the master potter. After a meal of roast chicken and three glasses of beer, I came out and lay on a twine cot under a green *neem* tree. Its bitter herbal foliage swayed, giving me a cool medicinal massage. I slept heavily.

The sun filtering through the leaves hit my eyes. I woke up, wondering where I was. I had momentarily lost all sense of direction and locale.

I bid goodbye to my friend and hurried home because I had locked the outer door and sent my servant to buy clay *divas*, crackers, and sparklers for the evening. Like most Indians, my mother believed that Lakshmi, the goddess of wealth, visits every home on Diwali night. The lamps must be lit and the doors kept open otherwise the goddess goes away.

On reaching my house I found that there was no padlock on the door. I wondered what had happened. A thief? Burglary was a common occurrence. There were a number of mechanics, locksmiths, and cobblers in the area. Though I had nothing valuable, my house had been burgled twice. The thieves had taken an old suede jacket and a blanket, scattering books, papers and negatives on the floor.

I knocked on the door. No response. I thumped again. I heard the latch click. The door opened. Amrita Pritam stood there, a honey-coloured shawl thrown carelessly over her shoulders. It had been almost a year since I had last seen her.

"When did you come from Bombay?" I asked as I hugged her.

"This morning. I sat on the platform with my two suitcases ... thinking, wondering where to go. I have left Bombay. It was horrible there. That fellow ... that Imroz ... jealous and possessive ... he reduced me to a domestic drudge. I was lugging a shopping bag, buying oranges, potatoes and eggs from the corner store ... walking in the sultry heat of Bombay ... exhausted ... cooking for him on a small charcoal-fed *angeethi*, in a little room ... all my money gone ... my car ... I'm ruined."

She started sobbing. "The whole of Delhi looks *ajnabi* ... every house shut for me. I thought of you, took a taxi and came here."

"How did you get in?"

She wiped her tears and regained her breath.

"I waited at your door for a little while. Then asked some people about you and told them that I was your guest ... that I am Amrita Pritam. But nobody knew me. I asked a locksmith across the lane to help me. He hesitated. But when I told him that I was your relative from Bombay, he used his bunch of keys and opened the lock. I came in and closed the door. I roamed your house, your kitchen, courtyard, the rooms ... I am grateful."

Meanwhile my servant returned with the Diwali purchases.

In the evening Amrita rolled cotton wicks, filled the *divas* with oil, and lighted them.

"People say Lakshmi comes to the house on Diwali night. Instead a pauper has come to your house." She broke into laughter.

T hose days my house had two little rooms. Years later, my painter-friend Satish Gujral visited my house and said, "Demolish this stupid wall. It's killing space. Make it one room ... a long room with a section of the little wall to give a feeling of division but also of space. By demolishing, you create beauty. Half of Delhi should be demolished. And you will have a better Delhi. They are not building Delhi. They are creating slums. Ugly pockets ... eyesores ..."

My studio-cum-bedroom became beautiful and cozy. This was probably Satish"s first architectural assignment.

Amrita had been under great mental strain throughout her train journey; sleepless, worried, tortured. She had not known where to go and what to do. Now she sparkled and laughed.

I put her bed in the adjoining room and she retired for the night.

In the morning the servant brought tea. I asked him to wake up Amrita.

After a while, Amrita joined me.

She told me that she had felt a stranger in Bombay. Her life was confined to a little room where she cooked and served Imroz. He fell ill and did not go to work. All the money melted away. He would lose his temper, sulk, taunt her and feel jealous of everybody. From a lover he became a husband. Cruel and impossible. "The very institution of marriage is hell," she said. "A man changes ... a woman becomes his possession. His property. I have always hated this."

"Where is he now?"

"In Bombay. I am through with this relationship. I don't know where I'll live. A woman needs a roof over her head, a house ... the keys of the house, of her almirah, her bedroom ..."

"Don't worry. I'll move to a friend's house. You can stay here till you are organised."

I heard a loud knock on the outside door, a frantic ringing of the bell.

It was Imroz.

He stood there in a thin woollen shawl, his face flushed, shivering and perspiring. He had high fever and two days' stubble. He asked me if he could come in. His suitcase was in the taxi.

I told my servant to bring in the suitcase.

Amrita saw him and hurriedly went into her room.

Imroz staggered into my room. I helped him lie on the bed and gave him a blanket. He heaved a sigh. "I have followed her in illness and high fever. I'm shattered."

I went to Amrita and asked her to meet him. She appeared afraid and nervous, and refused to meet him.

"Please. I don't want to meet him."

I returned to the ailing Imroz and sat by his side. He said that he had typhoid or some intestinal trouble and had constant fever and could not go to work. Was it his fault?

He loved her, but in his illness he had become a burden. What could he do? Instead of he looking after her, she was looking after him. The reversal of the roles had destroyed them.

He went on speaking about his illness and his dream of working, painting and creating, earning money and paying debts.

I called a doctor who examined him and prescribed medicine. I went out to buy the medicine, wondering about human relationships. How fragile.

I entered the courtyard with the medicine and found Amrita sitting on the floor talking to Imroz in a high-pitched voice, he replying in a shivering tone. I retraced my steps. I felt I was entering a forbidden temple. I went out and roamed Janpath.

When I returned, the house was calm. Imroz was lying in bed, and Amrita was in the other room.

I gave Imroz the medicine. In the evening the fever went

down. He was still weak and his pulse low, his body wet and clammy. He said weakly, "I'll go back to Bombay tomorrow morning. She doesn't want me. I followed her, but it's no use. She is stubborn. Anyway, I cannot stay here. It's hell to know that she is in the other room and won't talk to me. I'll go back."

The following morning I saw Imroz off at the railway station. He sat in the 2nd class in the Punjab Mail, and as the train moved off he waved his weak hand at me through the window.

When I returned, Amrita asked me, "Has he gone?"

"Yes"

"You saw him off?"

"Yes"

"Sure he has gone?"

"Yes"

"Good!" She heaved a sigh of relief. "I was afraid he wouldn't go. A big burden off my chest."

That afternoon her children came and begged her to return to her husband's home. But she refused.

In the evening she talked about her homelessness again. "A woman cannot be on the street. She needs a home."

That evening I left for Bhatinda where I had some urgent family business.

When I returned after three days, Amrita had left. I learnt from friends that she had gone with her children to her house in Patel Nagar.

A few months rolled by.

There was an international peace conference to mourn the African leader Patrice Lumumba who had been shot dead by an imperialist bullet. Writers from all over India had gathered to pass resolutions against this brutal murder, and wrote poems on Lumumba.

In the evening a poetical symposium was held in the Ram Lila grounds. Firaq Gorakhpuri presided. Ali Sardar Jafri, Mulk Raj Anand, Sahir, Khwaja Ahmed Abbas, Sajjad Zaheer and many celebrities attended. Amrita came to the function and sat near me on the dais.

She leaned over and said, "I hear he is in town. I'm afraid of him. He might come here. I've the feeling he will come. I see his image hovering. I think ..."

"You are imagining things. No one dare touch you."

After the *mushaira* was over, Jafri, Mulk, Amrita and I walked across the lawn in the evening shadows. Suddenly somebody came from behind and grabbed Amrita's arm and tried to drag her away. It was Imroz. She resisted, but he would not let go of her arm.

"What is this? He is molesting her!" I said.

Jafri smiled, "It's the *qissa of aashiq aur mashooq*. (A quarrel between the lover and the beloved.) We cannot interfere."

We walked on, discussing the poignant beauty of Sahir's poem on the theme of violence.

I saw Amrita and Imroz disappear in the dark.

M onths later I learnt that Amrita had sold her Patel Nagar house, collected advance royalties from publishers, pooled all her savings, and started building a house in Hauz Khas. She stayed there alone in a small room, supervising the construction brick by brick. At night when jackals howled, she would illuminate her little room with a lamp and write poetry.

I had gone to America. When I returned, she met me and said, "I have built my house. It's beautiful. Will you come and see me?"

I went to see her. A lone house in that desolate area. It had a brightly painted small iron gate, with her name plate on one side. She showed me the sitting room, her work room and dining room, explaining the function of each. There were large paintings of her own image in orange and black on the walls, inscriptions of her poems in beautiful calligraphy, and painted lampshades.

Pointing to a large lacquered black door, she said, "And this is his room. I'll call him."

She opened the door.

Imroz had a brush in his hand. He was busy painting a cover for her book.

He was the same bashful young painter, embarrassed and shy, as Amrita held his hand.

8

I had invited Khushwant Singh, the novelist journalist, Sham Lal, the Resident Editor of *The Times of India,* and a doctor-friend with their wives to an evening meal. I asked the servant to buy three chickens from the market.

It was the month of May 1964. My room was burning hot. I went to the Cottage Emporium to enjoy its air-conditioned cool, and wandered to the toy section of stuffed elephants, horses village brides. The electricity failed and it became stuffy and hot. I saw a group of people surrounding somebody, muttering. "It's terrible ... how could he? It's hot. Let's go out ... so hot ... how could Panditji ..."

A woman said, "Panditji has died."

I knew a Panditji at the cash counter who always greeted

the customers with a smile.

"How..?" I asked.

"Just now the radio has flashed the news. He is no more."

It was Pandit Jawaharlal Nehru.

There was commotion in the Emporium. I came out. People were closing their shops. I hurried home.

The cook had salted the chickens and was crushing *masala* seeds on a stone slab in preparation for the evening meal.

I checked with Khushwant Singh. He said he would not be able to come for dinner. Sham Lal also declined. A war of succession had started as to who would inherit the throne. I cancelled the dinner.

As evening fell and it became dark, I felt lonely in the house. The cook had gone, leaving a potful of chicken, spiced and roasted.

As I had no fridge, I started worrying about the chicken. It would go waste. I thought of inviting some friends for pot-luck. I locked the door and walked over to the tented coffee house where writers and poets always sat gossiping. I found the poet Tara Singh Kamil, the story writer Gulzar Singh, and a struggler, Krishanjit Singh, sitting around a table. I invited them to dinner.

They were happy at the mention of "roast chicken".

On the way Gulzar purchased a bottle of whiskey and some fish.

Reaching home, I found the door unlocked and a light on in my room. I thought perhaps I had left it that way. Gulzar put the fish and bottle down and said, "Let's drink in the courtyard under the flowering champak. Bring glasses! Let's celebrate the day."

Suddenly the light in my room went out. Who was in the

room?

"Come out, bastard! Come out!" Tara Singh shouted.

There was silence in the room.

Gulzar bellowed, "Come out, you crook! Sister-fucker!"

He went to the verandah, kicked the door open and put on the light.

A puny man in a chequered *lungi* and tattered shirt crouched in a corner. He was in his forties, with sunken cheeks and a sparse black beard. He was a thief come to steal in my absence. My friends guffawed on seeing him.

Tara Singh looked at him with contempt. "Don't you know it's a writer's house? There's nothing to steal here except books, manuscripts, pictures, old shoes and a tooth brush. What did you expect to find here? An elephant? Jewels? Gold? Dollars? Huh! You seem to be a fresher. Come out!"

The man was trembling. He slowly got up and folded his hands, "Pardon me *huzoor*. Have mercy on me. May Allah —"

Gulzar slapped him and he fell to the ground, howling. "Don't drag your Allah into our business. You—a Muslim? And a thief! It seems you are newly initiated in the art of stealing."

He ordered the thief to sit quietly in the courtyard as we started drinking.

Tara Singh tore a piece of fish and tossed it to him. "Eat it, rat! We share our food even with thieves. We love sharing. We are poets. Do you understand? Enjoy this little morsel before you are handed over to the police."

The thief caught the tossed fish in both hands, raised it to his forehead and started nibbling it.

Tara Singh emptied his glass in three big gulps, wiped his lips with his shirt sleeve and said, "The police and thief are strange bed-fellows. Both are prisoners of each other. Both tied to the same iron chain."

After some time I phoned the police. A sub-inspector and two constables came. The sub-inspector ordered the constables to search the thief's pockets. They found a sharp knife and a master key.

"Any other weapon? Search the room!"

They spotted a long spiked rod which the thief had left in the room. The inspector gave him two stinging slaps and the thief fell on his knees crying. "I never stole anything., *huzoor* ... my children are hungry ... I'm in search of a job ... hungry *huzoor* ... two children ..."

The sub-inspector grabbed him by the neck and kicked him. "Stop howling, bastard! Telling lies. All of you tell the same tale. Take him out and wait for me."

The constables dragged the thief away.

The sub-inspector looked around, cleared his throat and said, "Look, he has not committed any theft in the eyes of the law. He stole nothing. Let me explain. If a man takes out a sword and brandishes it, you cannot arrest him for murder. He may have the intention, but you'll have to prove even that. Some solid proof. Have you anything worth stealing in your house? I mean something which a thief can remove and sell."

I looked at him, puzzled. My books ... a straw basket ... wooden divan ... a second-hand ceiling fan ... mats ... clothes ... a typewriter I had purchased in Bombay's flea market.

The sub-inspector looked through the rooms to find some object with which he would incriminate the thief. He found a new Singer sewing machine which Krishanjit had purchased and left in my house that very morning to take to his village for his aunt. It had the receipt and the tag. A mock drama was enacted. The thief was made to carry the sewing machine on his head, walk in the service lane, and was arrested in the presence of two passersby as witnesses and taken to the police station.

We filled our glasses and raised a toast to Pandit Nehru.

"Nehru was a great man. We are left in wilderness. No one can replace him." Gulzar ruminated.

Tara Singh took a large gulp and blinked through his thick-lensed spectacles. "Nehru? Which Nehru? We are living in Gulzari Lal Nanda's era. Nehru died 4,000 years ago ... so distant and far away ... in the stone age ... iron age ... he is a thing of the past. We are living in a new era. Don"t talk about Nehru. He's gone. He doesn't exist. Let's talk about new times ... new dawn ... new people ..."

Gulzar's eyes blurred. His mouth twitched and he started weeping. Wiping his eyes, he suddenly started laughing. "I've shed my share of tears for Nehru. Now let's listen to Tara Singh"s poetry ... his new poem."

"You won't understand my poem" Tara Singh growled. "Firstly, tell me what's poetry? Do you know what poetry is?"

"Yes ... but I cannot define it. Can you? Tell me, what's water? What's sky? What's a rat? ... Cat ... ? Bat ...?"

"Fool! A statement of truth is not poetry. Poetry is illogical. If I write ... the sky is blue ... the birds are warbling ... the clouds are rumbling ... bullshit ! My poetry says that the sky is green ... milk is black ... snow is red ... the stunted tree is sitting like a humped camel! That's poetry. Do you understand?"

Gulzar's mind was in a groove. He repeated, "Nehru was a noble man ... a great man!"

Krishanjit was worried about his sewing machine. He broke into a Punjabi folk song: *Pakkay pul te laraian hoian, chhavian de kil tut gai.* (A battle took place on the stone bridge, the swords clanged, sparks flew and their handles broke).

"Nehru is dead. Now three thousand poems will be written on him," said Tara Singh. "The radio rate is rupees twenty-five per poem. I'll write three poems. Really bad poems, because they sell on the radio."

"Nehru was great. Life is great. We are great ... living ... breathing ..." mumbled Gulzar.

"Who cares what happens when we are dead. The slogans of *Save Motherland! Save Fatherland!* are to turn the youth into cannon-fodder. To die. To be butchered. To be heroes. Martyrs. Glorified in books to inspire the new generation to march 'into the jaws of death.' Have you ever seen a senator or a Member of Parliament picking up a rifle and going to the front to die in a trench? Never. It's a conspiracy of the middle-aged paunchy politicians to kill the youth."

He emptied his glass, and filled it again, speaking non-stop. "If they told me that a Taj Mahal would be built on my body, I would kick the Taj Mahal and say 'Give me a hut. Now! I don't care what happens after I die.' I can say that I was Shakespeare ... I can imagine that I am dead and see my dead self in the form of a ... I don't know what I am saying. Let me clear my thoughts. Well, who knows what's after death. It's only a fantasy, a foolish thought that one's name will live. What good is that to me? Now Nehru has died, but if they were to ask a young beggar to lie in State in place of Nehru and ask Nehru to change roles, I am sure Nehru would opt for living, and the beggar would refuse a State burial."

We sat drinking till midnight.

After my friends staggered out, the courtyard appeared barren. Only empty bottles on the floor, left-over bones and soiled leaf-cups.

I sat alone under the starry sky musing about life and death...

Where does our spirit go? Our soul? Is there a soul? Or just ashes and ruins? I have visited historical ruins ... broken monuments of Sultans ... tall weeds growing and pigs and donkeys urinating on their tombs ... Mughal princesses sleeping under the rubble ... this was their glory.

9

I finished my book on Indian theatre and mailed the manuscript to New Directions, New York. My first introduction to Garcia Lorca's plays and Pablo Neruda's poems had been through this publishing house, owned by James Laughlin, a wealthy aesthete and owner of a vast estate. New Directions tossed my manuscript to their drama wing, Theatre Art Books, run by two sprucely-dressed old bachelors, Robert McGregor and George, a Buddhist. They accepted the manuscript and sent me a contract with an advance of two hundred dollars. I was thrilled by the offer. They invited me to the release of my book and sent me an air ticket. I applied for an American Visa, filling countless forms, my background, purpose, affiliation, financial guarantees, etc.

After three weeks, I received a letter from the Visa Counsellor, Mr. Stork, asking me to see him. I reached Consulate at the appointed time. A junior officer conducted me through the clinical corridors and opened the door. I entered and heard the rustle of the heavily padded mahogany door closing behind me. Mr. Stork sat upright in his chair, his blond hair close-cropped, his face well-shaved. He asked me to sit down and started shuffling through some pink and yellow sheets. His face had a dour expression.

I gave him a friendly smile, which he ignored. He looked at me with a sullen penetrating gaze.

"How are you doing?" he asked

"Fine. I'm just packing and organising things to leave for the States."

"I'm not going to give you a visa, Mr. Gargi. I have called you today only to ask you a few questions about your background and activities. I would like to know your affiliations."

"I'm a member of the Sahitya Akademy Board. Executive member of the Sangeet Natak Akademy. I have received many awards for my books. My plays have been staged, broadcast, published and prescribed as textbooks in universities."

He snapped, "Let's come to the point! Have you ever taken part in a communist-sponsored peace movement?"

I knew what was coming. Regaining my cool, I said, "Well ... I did sign the peace appeal and took part in some rallies."

"Are you the a member of the Communist Party?"

"No."

"Have you been to Russia?"

"Yes."

"How many times?"

"Three times".

"Who financed you?"

"The Soviet Writers' Union invited me. In 1959, my play was staged by the Gypsy Theatre, Moscow. They sent me an invitation."

"Do you write for Russian papers?"

"Yes."

"How much money have you received so far?"

"Just my royalties. I live on my writing. I have also received royalties from French and German papers. Also from my New York publisher."

"Have you written for *The Soviet Land?*"

"Yes. I wrote only one article. Then stopped."

"Why?"

"Because they do not pay much."

A sardonic smile appeared on his lips and he thumbed through the yellow sheets again.

"Have you written any article against America?"

I kept silent.

"Did you write a play called *Rice Shoots* describing Americans as butchers in the Korean war?"

"Yes."

"Why?"

"I don't think it is wrong to write against war ... I am critical of my own country. I write against India's corruption, greed, the rotten system, and social and political ills."

"Have you written any article against Russia?"

I gave him a brief account of my first trip to Moscow in 1954. Khrushchev's six-hour speech at the 20th Congress Communist Party listing Stalin's atrocities. The Hungarian upsurge, Soviet tanks roaring in ... my change of attitude.

"When did your conversion take place?"

"No conversion. If I had swung to the other extreme that

too would have been politics."

"So you didn't take part in any communist activity after the Hungarian revolution?"

"No."

"Sure?"

"Yes!"

"When did you last take part in a peace rally?"

"Well ... I didn't take part in the Peace Movement after 1957. I don't think ..."

"Lies!". He thumped the table, his steely blue eyes emitting sparks. "You are a liar!"

The word LIAR burst like a cracker. Hot blood coursed through my body. I sat speechless. He continued in a stern voice, "You were a delegate at the World Peace Conference in Delhi last month. You are a liar."

A million thoughts flashed in my head. Suddenly I remembered that I had gone to see a Tagore play staged at Vigyan Bhavan by the World Peace Council. I had had to pay two rupees as entry fee, which the organisers were collecting from the delegates. I did not even know that I was a delegate.

I explained this to Stork, but he rejected my plea with disdain.

I related my story to Satish Gujral, who was very friendly with the Cultural Counsellor Tom Noonan, a theatre lover and a puppeteer.

At a dinner at his house Satish commented on America's cultural policy and said to Tom, "You Americans are fools! You have no vision. Always suffering from a self-persecution mania. Writers in India are left-wing but it does not mean that they are anti-American. Look at me. I have been a leftist throughout. My paintings on Partition speak against the horrors of war, human misery, blood and killing. This could be related to the Vietnam war. You allow all sorts of crooks, gamblers, bastards, criminals and prostitutes to land in America. Why not Balwant Gargi? I have known Balwant for the last fifteen years and we have been close friends. He is no communist. Hardly even a socialist. He is just a writer!"

A month later, Tom directed Anouilh's *The Lark* for the American Embassy. Ironically Stork played the Inquisitor. After the show I congratulated Tom and Stork for their production and excellent performance. I don't know what happened. Maybe my New York publishers had pulled some strings. Or Stork had a change of mind. I received a phone call from him, asking me to apply again for a visa. I filled up the form. There was a clause in the proforma 'Has your application for a visa ever been rejected?' I had heard that once a visa is rejected, they seldom grant it. I wrote in the box 'Yes.'

Within fifteen days I got my visa.

In New York I stayed with the Jewish intellectual Ralph Berens, an assistant editor in *The New York Times*. He lived on Third Avenue and 36th Street between the two giant skyscrapers of The Chryseler and Empire State buildings.

New York was no surprise to me. Its skyscrapers were exactly the same as I had seen in pictures. In fact they did not look all that tall. Manhattan, a fish-shaped island, the world's capital of business and art, is divided into parallel broad avenues cut by nearly 150 streets into tall cubes. It is easier to walk to a place than go by cab in the choked traffic. Very few can afford a car because of the high parking charges. Everyone walks, pushing, jostling, rushing. You can recognise a New Yorker by his gait.

I always seek a theatre or a cafe when I visit a new city. A gleaming McDonald's did not attract me. It was neat, smooth, and trashy. I stumbled into Greenwich Village with its crazy little lanes lined with curio shops, art galleries and cafes, the haunt of sleazy actors, painters, dancers and jobless artists. Here, coffee was fifty cents a cup. Chairs and tables had a sheen of over-use. People played chess or smoked and sat for hours. I used to sit here over coffee, writing letters, watching people.

One day Ralph had gone to work leaving me with the keys of his double-locked apartment. He was to return in the evening. He told me to lock the door securely, as there had been robberies. I was not to open the door without looking through the peephole and hearing the person's voice. I roamed about the apartment, wandered to the kitchen, had tea and sat down to write a letter. I heard footsteps and a rumbling voice on the stairs. I wondered who was coming up, mine being the top floor of that old building. I peeped through the 'crystal eye'. A heavy-jowled black drunk had tottered up and was trying to open his apartment door, fumbling with his key.

I returned to my letter-writing. Suddenly I felt the urge to go to an Italian cafe on the street corner and have an espresso.

I inserted the key to open the lock but it would not open. I tried both keys several times. Thumped on the door. Shouted. Again tried the keys and hammered on the door. The sound echoed down the empty wooden stairs but nobody came to my help. I had forgotten to take the telephone number of my host. Perspiring and dizzy, I examined the keys again, their little notches, fixed them carefully in the keyhole and juggled the knob, but the door did not open.

I was Qasim in the cave of the Forty Thieves and had forgotten the magic words, "Open Sesame."

The room became a suffocating tomb. Deathly walls. The

space shrank and paralysed me. I started panting. I lay on the couch breathing heavily ... rest ... rest ... but my mind was in a whirl ... suppose my host did not return at five ... he might go to a movie ... or to his country house for the weekend ... I might die.

In a fit of desperation, I tried the keys again. They turned with a click and the door opened. I stood there, contemplating my freedom. Years ago I had experienced the same claustrophobic feeling when Nehru's Government had refused me a passport.

Ralph invited two of his colleagues to dinner. One with a short brown moustache looked after the Arts section, and the other, a woman with heavy silken hair, was on the literary desk.

While discussing the political situation in India, its economy, poverty and writers, I asked them which Indian writers they liked. They listed R.K. Narayan, Naipaul, Ruth Jhabwala, Ved Mehta, etc.

"Do you know any of our great writers and poets? Have you heard the name of Saadat Hasan Manto, the famous Urdu short story writer? The novelist Saratchandra Chatterjee? Prem Chand? Iqbal?"

Ralph and his colleagues drew a blank. They had never heard of these names. "We know only those who write in English."

"But they are not our best writers. Most Indians writing in English are mediocre. Our greatest writers are in our regional languages. Manto can be compared with Chekhov or Maupassant. Iqbal was a world genius!"

The arts editor said, "We don't know them. For us they

do not exist."

"What do you mean?"

"Anything that is not in English is unknown to us. It does not exist for us."

"So if someone does not know that an American astronaut walked on the moon, does it mean that this fact is not a reality?"

"Your writers may be great, but who knows them?" Said the literary editor. "They are like pearls hidden in the depths of dark oceans ... diamonds buried deep in the bowels of a mountain. They have no reality."

The arts editor added, "Many stars bigger than the sun roam in space but are so distant that the human eye cannot detect them. These stars simply do not exist."

I was startled by their logic. For the Western world Iqbal did not exist. Nor Manto. Nor Kabir, nor Ghalib, nor Kalidasa.

The dinner was over at a dead end.

M y publisher asked me if I would like to meet some theatre personalities. He would organise a dinner for the occasion.

"Only two persons", I said. "Elia Kazan and Tennessee Williams."

He looked doubtful. "Tennessee is ill. Just now he is in Florida. If he comes to New York, we'll try to arrange a meeting with him. But Elia Kazan—it's difficult to reach him."

I contacted Miss Ross Glider, 'grandmother' of the American theatre whom I had met during her visits to India. She treated me to dinner in her apartment. A squat spinster in her eighties she had a crystal-clear mind and resonant voice. "Tennessee used to come here and sit in that chair", she reminisced "...like a schoolboy ... a gifted writer, always tortured by success and failure. I have very little contact with him now. And with Elia Kazan ... none."

I came back disappointed.

I had heard of Elia's bad temper. He abhorred flowery oriental courtesies and compliments.

I gave up the idea of seeing him.

One morning I was awakened by Ralph. "Balwant! A call for you from Elia Kazan."

I took the telephone. Elia's secretary was on the line. "Your meeting with Elia has been fixed for six p.m. today in his office on Broadway. Do you confirm it?"

Elated, I said, "Yes."

I wondered how it had happened. Later I learned that Miss Ross had fixed it.

Ten minutes later there was another phone call from Paul Mann, a burly actor who ran a small studio theatre to train actors, and was working in Elia's film. He said in his booming voice that I should be in his studio at five sharp. He would brief me on the meeting with Elia and would take me to him.

I was with him at the appointed hour. He sat in a deep chair, his foot bandaged, stick in hand. His eyes were a shining green. He extended his hand, told me sit down, and began a lecture on the cut-throat theatre world of New York.

"The glitter of Broadway has ruined good art and theatre. Elia Kazan is no exception. He is very greedy and calculating. Look at me. I am working in his film *America, America*. But I'm being paid only five thousand dollars, peanuts for an actor like me."

He cleared his throat, rolled his green eyes and said, "You are an important playwright from India. We need you. Elia wants to meet you. After all, India is a great country. Otherwise why would he meet you? I have arranged this meeting by selling you ... In America, we have to sell things. Even to be a playwright, you have to be a salesman. Don't be taken in by Elia's gushing handshakes and sweet talk. You are an important personality ... he needs you."

"Paul, you have done me a great wrong, " I said. "I am just a playwright in a regional language ... a nobody here. I am Elia's fan. I want to meet him. I have seen most of his films, which are now classics, and also know a lot about his theatre productions and his creative direction of Tennessee Williams' plays ... specially *A Street Car Named Desire* and *Cat on a Hot Tin Roof*.

"Don't talk about Tennessee Williams to him. They hate each other. Just talk about your own work ... now come. We must be on time. His office is across the street."

Paul rose and limped ahead of me with his bandaged foot. We crossed the street, took a lift and reached Elia's office. Paul stood outside the office, looking at his watch. At six sharp, he pressed the bell and walked in.

The receptionist said, "Mr. Kazan is on a long-distance call. Please wait a few minutes."

I wandered into the room and looked at the posters of *A Street Car Named Desire,* and *Cat on a Hot Tin Roof*.

Suddenly a hairy hand grabbed me. "Come!" said Paul.

The secretary led us into Elia's room. He sat reclining on a sofa in his pet pose which I had seen in countless photographs. He stood up with the agility of a leopard, came up to me, extended his hand and shook mine in welcome.

We sat down across a table. "What'll you have? Whiskey, coffee or ...?"

"Coffee," I mumbled. Elia asked his secretary to send two coffees and one Scotch.

"What are you doing in New York?" He shot at me. I was

tongue-tied.

He stirred his Scotch, took a gulp and again asked, "What brings you to New York?"

I did not know what to say. I spoke about my theatre book ... New York's artistic and money power ... something... I don't remember what.

"Every bastard wants dollars in this fucking country. Look at this son of a bitch! I paid him five thousand dollars for a little role, but he is always bitching. I tell him to take it or leave it. Don't waste my time. He doesn't deserve even that."

I had forgotten about Paul's presence. Elia spoke to me keeping Paul out of frame. I realised that Paul had tried to sell me to Elia by constantly condemning American salesmanship, commercial values, and hunger for money. His briefing had frozen me. My conversation became artificial and stupid. I shrugged off his instructions., I asked Elia. "Why have you stopped directing Tennessee Williams' plays?"

He smiled. "Well, Tennessee is a talented playwright. I love his writing, full of tenderness and passion ... beautiful images ... We've often differed in the structure of a scene. We had a thundering argument over the end scene of *Cat on a Hot Tin Roof*. I insisted on my version. The play is published with two versions of the last act, offering the reader a choice. Maybe his third act is good literature but mine is good theatre. Now, I am not interested in Broadway any more. Goodbye commercial theatre! I want to write a novel."

We talked of India, its films and arts, Mughal architecture, and the teeming street life he had seen in pictures. Suddenly he said, "I like your Ray. A great director. Tell him that I am his fan. When are you returning to India?"

"In October".

"I'll be shooting *America, America* in Athens at that time.

Would you like to stop over at Athens? Be my guest for three days. I'll treat you to delicious Greek food. Also a wench to sleep with. Will you come?"

"I'd love to."

He pressed the button. His secretary appeared. He told her the schedule.

He looked at his watch and said, "Come again or ring me up. I would like you to meet my wife. Now I have to go."

In the corridor Paul said, "You didn't talk about me to Elia. You've seen how blunt and money-minded he is. I'm on sale. My price is much more. But he won't give it to me. See what New York does to people? Tfoo!"

From New York I went to London in August, stayed there for two months, met old friends, saw new plays, wandered the familiar streets and booked my seat back home via Athens. I arrived in the ancient city, took a small hotel room and telephoned Elia.

The manager told me that Elia had left for shooting very early. In the evening I rang up again. I was told that Elia was tired and had gone to bed.

I left a message and my telephone number.

I went out in a tourist bus, visiting historical places. The guide was a retired professor of art history who loved to impart knowledge. I spent an afternoon at the Acropolis and the Parthenon. Pointing to a high frieze, the professor said, "A part of this frieze was stolen by Lord Elgin. It's now preserved in British Museum. We are trying to get it back. But the British won't give it to us."

I had seen the missing part of the frieze in the British

Museum. A note at bottom had said that the other part was in Athens at the Parthenon. I pieced the two together in my mind and saw them as one.

In the evening Elia took me to a Greek dinner. With him was a famous local poet. We wandered through the open-air restaurants dotting the slopes of the Acropolis. He chose his favourite restaurant. The owner welcomed him with a hug. We sat down at the table. Elia went to the open-air kitchen, lifted the lid of each metal pot, inhaling whiffs of steaming *biryani* and meat curries. He returned and said, "Always look at the food by lifting the lid. You can always judge a woman or food this way."

While having dinner, we talked about his film. I asked him which Hollywood actor was playing the main role. "To hell with Hollywood!" he said. "No American actor, but one from Greece. A twenty-one-year-old Greek boy. He appeared at my Manhattan office and begged for a role. I was struck by his passion. He had worked his way in a ship to New York to reach me. You need passion to work in films. You can't flirt with this medium. You have to be damn serious. It's an all consuming mistress. Very demanding."

"Would you like to act in my film?" he asked me suddenly.

"Are you serious."

He explained the scene to me, "There are 20 passengers in a boat—Asians, Arabs, Turks, Negroes, and one Indian in a dhoti, a doctor. As the boat wobbles, they roll over each other and shriek in confused tongues. You'll play the doctor."

"Have I to speak some lines?"

"Yes. I'll write them down just now."

He grabbed a paper napkin and wrote.

"Hai Rama! Save me! It's hell! Save me! It's hell! Save me! I am drowning. Help!"

All night I nervously tried to memorise the lines. I couldn't sleep.

In the morning his secretary came in a car. After an hour's drive through orange and olive groves we reached the spot. Elia was directing a shot in the burning sun and had taken off his shirt. He was perspiring, ordering the cameraman and the actors.

The secretary hurriedly passed me on to the wardrobe assistant, who handed me a turban and a *sherwani* to wear for the role. I refused, on the pretext that this costume did not suit the role. I couldn't face the camera. It was easier to face a gun.

I fled.

10

My cook Kishori Lal, his wife Mangala and their three sons lived in a tiny room of nine feet by six feet. This cubicle was attached to my courtyard, separated by a wall.

Mangala, a hill woman, was slim, fair complexioned and had luxurious black hair. On her left arm was tatooed a green cobra, guardian of the underworld. She cooked, washed, scrubbed, stitched and supervised her sons' homework. Their entire household possessions—utensils, tin trunks, straw mats, clothes, bundles—were arranged at various levels. Some hung from the ceiling, some were in racks and some were under the bed. If Kishori was not there and the door-bell rang, Mangala would open the door and welcome the visitor with a smile. Everything was neat and pure. I never heard any argument between Kishori Lal and Mangala. Their conversations, emotions, and movements were rubber-soled.

In my courtyard there was a stone statue of Ganesha. Mangala lit the worship lamp daily, garlanded the elephant-headed god and mumbled mantras to the deity. On festivals she would place a banana and sweets before Ganesha, which made the god come to life. The stone image breathed.

Living in this little room Kishori managed to save some money, took a loan from relatives and purchased a tiny two-room house in a far-off colony. The area was five yards by five yards, four times larger than the cubby-hole they had been cooped up in for the past seven years.

They made preparations to move to their new house.

Kishori brought a tempo, loaded it with household objects and sat atop a tin trunk as the tempo rolled off. Mangala and the children went by bus. While leaving they bowed to Ganesha, bid me farewell with folded hands and looked at the little room with nostalgia.

I felt as if a large chunk of life had been ripped out of the courtyard. I had seldom conversed with them, but had always felt their warmth and presence. As the children chanted their lessons their voices would filter into the courtyard. The smell of hill food, spiced rice and fried beans floated in the air. There was a sense of life.

They slept with the door of their cabin closed. But I felt sensations of human beings transmitted to me. Now they were gone. The courtyard was empty. God Ganesha with his black trunk and broken tusks was cold. The marigold around his neck had withered. The oil had dried and the wick was dead. Life had been snuffed out in the niche. I double-bolted my door and went to bed.

I had read in the papers about murders of aged persons

living alone in posh localities of Delhi ... thefts and killings ...

Suddenly I heard mysterious sounds ... muffled noises ... rustles ... then a low hammering and metallic crackles. Perhaps someone was trying to open the lock. I switched on the light, came out and shouted, "*Oay, kaun hai?*"

Sweat broke on my brow and my legs went cold. Again I asked in a frightened croak, "Who is there?"

Silence fell in the courtyard. Everything became still ... the courtyard held its breath ... a frightening stillness ... perhaps a bandit was hiding in the bathroom ... or the kitchen ... My heart was thumping. I could hear it knocking against my ribs. I took courage and walked to the bathroom door and kicked it with all my force.

A cat jumped over the parapet of the low wall and disappeared. She had smelled the left-overs in the plastic dustbin in the kitchen, clambered upon the wall, and had been sitting on the parapet crunching bones.

I returned to my room and lay in my bed, wide awake. I felt the emptiness around me, a dark vacuum, space closing in on me ... I put on the lights. My eyes travelled to the walls ... Picasso's Blue Nude ... a woman hiding her head in her folded arms, her rippling body lines, the flesh tones done in blue ... a Gujral oil on a sawdust canvas ... green and vermilion streaks ... Urdu books calligraphed in crazy lines ... cracks in the wall ... I must get the walls repaired. Rains will be coming soon ... the roof may collapse. Suppose the roof fell on me ... I started calculating its weight ... could I wriggle out of the debris ... Could I shout 'Help!'

How was I living so long? Death is not a surprise. Life is. How was I able to live all these years ...? If a mosquito had bitten me intelligently, I would have died. Billions of germs in the air attacking my body system ... Murders, accidents, air crashes, riots, illness ... Yet I was breathing, thinking, living. A miracle!

Of late, I had been reading Maupassant, who described his loneliness ... the terror of being alone at night. Every object became different ... shadows changed and hovered and assumed personalities. He often returned late in the evenings to his bachelor apartment. Once he entered his room and saw a man sitting in the arm chair, silhouetted in the glow of the fireplace ... must be a friend come in his absence and taken the key from the landlady and sat there waiting and dozed off. Maupassant cleared his throat but the man was fast asleep, his hand resting on the arm chair. Maupassant tapped the man on the shoulder and jumped back. He had hit the wooden back of the chair.

He put on the light. There was nobody there.

Looking at myself I imagined I was another man. I wondered who this man was lying in bed ... breathing. I raised my hand and wondered at the movement — who was controlling it? Who am I? This body lying ... chest heaving. I looked at my arm again and allowed it to travel to my chest in slow motion, felt my heart, removed my hand and laid it on the bed ... the estranged arm lay by my side. I closed my eyes and tried to sleep.

I felt hollowed out ... I was dissolving in space, sinking in loneliness. I wanted to listen to some one breathing, some friend, a woman, a servant, a dog ... any one breathing and alive.

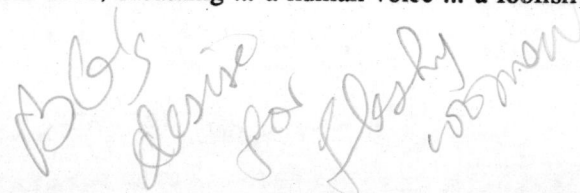

I knew women who were intelligent, beautiful, artistic and charming. But I did not want them. I wanted some earthy woman, plump, ugly, foolish, non-intellectual, but one who would reply when I called out in my frightened loneliness. Just someone breathing in the room. I did not seek love, but the mere presence of another human being. Some one to remind me that I was alive, breathing ... a human voice ... a foolish voice ...an ugly voice ... a plump voice.

Lying in bed, the thought of death haunted me ... nightmarish images ... disjointed arms and heads ... Suddenly the youthful face of Yukio Mishima appeared before my eyes ... the beauty and horror of his death.

I had met Mishima in 1962 in Tokyo on my way to New York. It was April, the month of cherry blossoms. Haiku poets celebrated death ...to die in the prime of youth ... gracefully, beautifully ... like cherry blossoms which fall in full bloom with grace and elegance.

I received a message from Mishima in my small hotel in Tokyo that he would be coming to take me out to lunch. The desk informed me that there was someone to see me. I came down and saw a boyish-looking muscular young man waiting for me in the foyer. It was Mishima—Japan's flamboyant playwright and novelist. I had read some of his stories and plays and was struck by their unusual power.

He gave a milky smile and shook my hand with a strong grip. Most Japanese give a broad smile which is more a mannerism than an expression of any emotion, the smile acting like a veil. But Mishima's smile was sunny and fresh, like a river of milk.

"I am Mishima," he said. "Are you Gargi? Good! Let's go."

He took me to a Chinese restaurant. A tall, slim old man with a wispy long beard and a gold-laced mandarin-collared kaftan greeted us. He led us to a table elegantly laid out with chopsticks and two large plates with dragons fired in green and red.

I had a bright blue Japanese paper napkin on my knees. I felt its rustle and silken texture, and did not dare wipe my hands with it because of its aesthetic beauty.

I heard 'Mishima ... Mishi ... hishi ...' People were whispering Mishima's name ... a wave of appreciation.

He ordered soup, shredded bamboo, lobster cooked in wine, and noodles flavoured with hot soya sauce. He spoke excitedly. "The Chinese taught us the art of cooking. We taught them the art of chivalry, which they never learnt. They handle chopsticks and we swords!" He laughed. "After Hiroshima, we were reduced to a pulp ... no food ... I went to the fields, dug out potatoes with my own hands and brought them home to cook. But in fifteen years we have rebuilt ourselves. It's not America, it's Japan. Japan's power to create, design, and our sense of pride. We have touched the depths of degradation. Now we'll rise to the highest glory. The Americans are destroying our culture. An evil influence. They are enemies of our imperial tradition .. its purity and culture."

Mishima asked for the bill. The mandarin apologised and said that it was an honour to have Mishima grace his retaurant. Three waitresses asked for his autograph. He sketched his name on their diaries smiling the same milky smile. One waitress lifted a corner of her skirt and spread it on the table. Mishima signed it.

That afternoon he took me to a performance of Kabuki. The large well-lit Kabuki-Za was heaving with a full house. I saw the beautifully painted front curtain and was amazed by its expensive silken sheen. I looked again. There was a new curtain with another painting on its silk spread. Again it was replaced by a third curtain with an exquisite painting. I asked : "Why are there so many front curtains?"

"These are advertisements. Look, there is the name of the advertiser down in the right corner, embroidered in fine lettering." He gave me his binoculars and I looked through them. "The advertisers spend millions on these silk curtains painted by top artists, and their names are hidden below in a corner. The publicity posters of the West shriek. The Kabuki would not allow such vulgarity."

I was surprised by the beauty of the decor and the well-dressed people, the women in kimonos with slit sleeves, their glossy hair piled high in flower-decked coiffures.

The festivity was due to the honouring of the Eleventh Danjuro as a national actor in the great Kabuaki tradition.

"He is our greatest actor today," Mishima said. "This honour is very frightening. One Danjuro was awarded this honour at the turn of the last century. When he learnt that his father had influenced the jury, he came home and committed hara-kiri to uphold the honour of the art of acting. If some day I find that a wrong is being done to my nation and nothing can stop it, I might commit hara-kiri." He laughed, a schoolboy's laughter.

Mishima was waging a war against America's domination. He believed that America had corrupted Japanese society and eroded its glory. At that time there were one hundred thousand 'rocket girls' in Tokyo serving drinks in hotels, soliciting customers, earning money from the flesh trade. American rock-and-roll and fast rhythms had torn apart the musical fabric of Japanese music. Mishima fought against it with his band of followers trained in martial arts, committed to the revival of Japan's imperial past.

In 1970, Mishima decided to avenge the shame and defeat America had inflicted on Japan. He rallied his disciples and stood on a high parapet shouting at the Japanese people to rise in revolt against American domination, but no one cared to listen to him. He made a fiery speech, yelled and committed the ritualistic hara-kiri by ripping open his abdomen with a sword. One of his disciples standing behind chopped off his head, and a second follower chopped off the first one's head, completing the doubel hara-kiri which sent shock waves throughout the world.

11

The Film Festival Directorate were trying to get Elia Kazan to participate in the Festival as a Jury Member. He was not traceable. They sent telegrams to the Indian Consulate in New York to contact the celebrity, offer him a first class air ticket and hospitality, sent a telegram to his agents, but there was no reply.

Someone told the Directorate that I knew Elia well and could be of help. I suggested to Deputy Director Urmila Gupta that the best way to reach Elia was to write him a letter. I gave her his country house address and telephone number.

Urmila sat down at the typewriter and I dictated a letter explaining to Elia the urgency and richness of the experience. It was important for him to attend the Festival.

After a week I received a telegram saying that he would

come, not as a member but as an observer. "Tell the Festival people to send me two air tickets—one for my wife".

Elia arrived in Delhi with his wife, the actress Barbara Loden, who maintained her maiden name even after marriage.

I had seen Barbara on the stage playing Marilyn Monroe in *After the Fall*, a bad play by Arthur Miller, which opened in New York in 1964. Elia had taken me to the performance and we sat to one side of the sixth row in a half-empty hall. Barbara glided on stage as the glamorous sex queen, bathed in milky light. Elia watched her avidly, seeing in her the beautiful Marilyn with whom he had a roaring affair. After the show he took me backstage and introduced me to Barbara as he hugged her for her "brilliant" performance.

Now after twelve years, Barbara had thinned and lost her voluptuous form. Elia and she went to the inauguration of the Festival, sat on the dais amidst other members, but made no speech. Next evening they came to my house for dinner.

Elia stood in the middle of the courtyard and looked at the sky, then at the arches of my little verandah. "It's very Greek ... rather Turkish ... it reminds me of my childhood. ..my village was under the Turks when I was a child." During dinner we discussed the Indian political scene and films. Barbara hardly spoke.

Elia said, "Tomorrow we won't be attending the viewing session. I can't suffer the boredom of watching bad films. Could you come to my hotel around nine? We shall go out. Barbara has her own programme. She is interested in jewellery, antiques and Buddhist philosophy. I'll be with you. We'll roam the old city lanes together."

"What did you do yesterday?"

"I went to a cremation ground and watched the dead burning. I inhaled their fumes. I think Hindus have the noblest ritual of burning the dead. Not like us barbarians. We put the body in a coffin and let it rot. To visualise that worms are eating the eyes of a dear one, or that a rodent is crunching the skull and gobbling bits of brain like pudding, gives me the creeps. Here, it's pure. Fire destroys everything, the good and the evil..."

The following day I went to fetch them in my little car. I had ripped off its steel top and turned it into a convertible. Barbara and Elia sat in this humpy beetle and I drove them through Connaught Place to Jama Masjid. We walked around the mosque and down the jewellery bazar. Merchants reclined against cotton-stuffed bolsters amidst their primitive weighing scales and ornaments. Barbara made some purchases after much haggling.

"I'll join you in front of the mosque on the steps." She said, and walked on.

Elia gave a wry smile, "Women can never make up their mind. Always unsure of themselves. A man spends half his life paying compliments to his wife, admiring her face, eyes, waist, legs, shoes. A sheer waste of time."

Inside the mosque, we wandered in the spacious red-stoned courtyard, looked at the high-vaulted arches of the sanctum sanctorum—the house of Allah—empty and beautiful. It was cold. The sun shivered behind a thick pall of smog and cast a pale light.

We walked down the steps into a lane thickly populated with Muslim shops of the old world. Steaming *biryani*, cauldrons of meat bubbling on flaming ovens, smoke-filled dingy shops. Hefty butchers hacking at hunks of the choicest meats. Beautifully calligraphed Qurans in shimmering green, women in black burqas sitting like huge cats on cycle rickshaws, their eyes blinking from behind squares of gauze. Beggars hobbling on crutches, seeking alms in the name of Allah.

Elia took out his note book and scribbled something in it. He remarked, "Those long-bearded fakirs look biblical. It's very restful here. These people remind me of my own village ... I would like to make a film on such people." A sweaty bald man in a long kaftan and green beads was arguing loudly with a shopkeeper. He saw Elia and turned to him *"Allah ka qahr hai! Iss aurat ne jeena haram kar diya!"*

I translated it. "Allah's wrath has fallen on us. This woman has made our life hell. She is a monster! She has crushed everyone. We cannot open our mouths ... cannot utter a single word. My heart is burning. We cannot breathe. She is a ruthless woman. A dictator!"

He was railing against Indira Gandhi.

Indira Gandhi had clamped Emergency. The press was muzzled. There was an uproar in the country. The Opposition had challenged her law by staging protest marches, burning buses and looting trains. Many were arrested. Indira had crushed the revolt with an iron hand. The rebellion simmered down.

The shaggy-bearded man shouted, *"Allah! yeh aurat to dictator hai!"*

Elia said to me, "Does this man know what a dictator is? Poor bastard. He has no idea." Then he turned to the man and asked, "How is it that you are speaking against her so openly in the bazaar! If she is a dictator and some one reports the matter..."

Walking with me, Elia said, "There was an outrage against Indira Gandhi in the US press. Some called her a dictator. But I find a great deal of freedom here. Your people have no idea what a dictator is. They can't imagine the terror of a Hitler. That midnight visit. That chilling knock ... your fate sealed for ever. Horror haunts your dreams. You start fearing the walls of your house. People in India have no idea of a dictator!"

12

I had moved to Chandigarh and set up the Department of Indian Theatre for the Panjab University. My house was located at the back of the Open Air Theatre, a fortress of ancient stones, where I taught and directed plays.

The telephone rang. I picked up the receiver and heard a flat cold voice, "I'm the Superintendent of Police speaking. Is it Professor Balwant Gargi?"

"Yes."

"We have an urgent business with you. We'd like to inspect your house."

"What for?"

"We cannot tell you. Stay in your house. We are coming." And he hung up.

My knees went limp. I have a fright of the police. Why was he coming to search my house? I hastily recalled all the possible crimes I might have committed even in my dreams. Why was the police after me?

The screech of a jeep startled me. I came out of the house. A burly police officer emerged and four constables jumped out. He walked up to me, "I'm the Superintendent of Police. Are you Balwant Gargi? I need to talk to you about something very important."

I led him into the drawing room and asked him to take a seat. He settled himself in a cane chair, cleared his throat and said, "We've received a flash message from Delhi. Madam Indira Gandhi is coming to your house. We want to inspect the site, the back lane, bushes, the far-off buildings. Security, you know? Madam will come to your house at four o'clock on January third and have tea with you. For thirty-five minutes. The maximum number of people at tea should not exceed fourteen. No VIPs. No Vice-Chancellor. No political leaders. Only artists, writers, painters, actors."

He shook hands with me and went out to scan the landscape with his team.

Joyfully, I gave this news to Jeannie who was baking waffles in the kitchen with her arm in plaster. She had been knocked down by a rushing motorcyclist on the road and had fractured her collarbone.

"Why is she coming to our house?" she asked.

I said, "Well ..."

Jeannie's face changed. Her golden-blue eyes turned steely grey. "But we cannot afford tea for fourteen people. We don't have money."

"But ... but it's the Prime Minister coming ... Indira Gandhi ..."

"Where is the money? On Christmas you had to borrow money to buy a turkey. No sponge cake ... no gifts for the children."

She argued and complained listing all items neglected so far in the house. She hated to borrow money. "Can't Indira Gandhi afford tea in her own house? We are under heavy debt."

Her absurd calculations annoyed me. Even if Jesus had come to the house, she would not have borrowed money to entertain Him. Seeing her trembling with financial worry, I held her hand, "Listen darling, It's like the US President ... or Queen Elizabeth coming to our house ... Indira Gandhi ... Why can't we afford tea for her? We won't make any elaborate arrangements. Simple tea. It won't cost much. We'll have a log fire. Mrs. Gandhi will sit on the cushioned divan. Actors, painters and writers on the carpeted floor. The girls will prepare and serve tea. You need not do anything. Just sit with her and smile. Or we could ask the Hospitality Department. Their liveried staff could serve *pakoras*, fried fish, *burfi* and tea. They charge only eleven rupees per head. An expense of one hundred and fifty rupees. The Theatre Department will foot the bill."

Jeannie finally agreed.

I rang up the Vice-Chancellor Suraj Bhan to give him the news. He was an arts promoter, fond of me, always helpful, and attended all my productions on the opening night. Now I found him suddenly cold. He said, "I don't know. See me tomorrow in my office at ten."

The following day he gave me a royal chewing. With his heavy face flushed, he asked me how I had reached Madam Gandhi. How could I bypass official regulations? Why was she coming to my house? How had I managed it?

I told him that she had come to see my play *Sultan Razia* which Alkazi had directed and produced in Delhi. I had met her then.

"Did you invite her to tea?"

"No."

"You mean to tell me that she is coming uninvited?"

"Yes."

"We have been trying to get her to the campus for the last eight months to inaugurate the Students Centre. She was busy. Now you tell me that she is coming to your house ... How?"

"Mr. Vice-Chancellor, if you have been trying to get her to the campus for the last eight months, do you think she would come to my house just for the asking?"

He glowered at me. "You must understand that you have many enemies here. The Dean tells me that you are going about arrogating that you have direct links with the Prime Minister. This will harm you. You should have invited her through the proper channels."

The campus was the Vice-Chancellor's dukedom. I realised that, after all, it was the Vice-Chancellor with whom I would have to deal. I had to seek his sanction for a holiday, sick leave, even for a bulb in my apartment. It was like living in a river and being at war with the crocodile.

I rang up Usha Bhagat, Social Secretary to Mrs. Gandhi, and requested her to talk to the Vice-Chancellor who was sulking in his house.

Usha rang him up. After ten minutes, the Vice-Chancellor called me, "I received a call from the Prime Minister's house just now. They have told me to make arrangements."

In the morning, he rang up the police chief and told him that the road leading to my house was not safe for Madam's visit. The venue was being changed to the Fine Arts quadrangle.

The police chief said that they could not change the venue unless Mr. Gargi agreed to it.

I surrendered.

The venue was changed. The seats were arranged in a large heated room, chairs lined up along the walls, two high-backed velvet cushioned chairs in the centre.

Indira Gandhi walked in with the Vice-Chancellor. The Dean pointed to the high-backed chairs. Mrs. Gandhi ignored him and sat down in a small chair. Jeannie sat by her side with her plastered arm in a sling.

Mrs. Gandhi looked around and called the artists and writers to sit near her. The dead floor came to life.

Suddenly I saw Chief Minister of Punjab Giani Zail Singh and Haryana Chief Minister Bansi Lal walking in. Mrs Gandhi looked at them, "Gianiji, occupy those chairs." They dutifully sat down in the royal chairs.

Zail Singh wore a badge inscribed: "I am Madam Indira Gandhi's devoted servant."

Mrs. Gandhi asked Jeannie about her fractured arm. Jeannie extended it to her and Mrs. Gandhi autographed the plaster.

After her arm healed, Jeannie removed the plaster shell and preserved it as a souvenir.

After a month I visited Delhi and came to know that Usha Bhagat had been enquiring about me. I rang her up. She said, "Where did you disappear? We searched for you everywhere. Phoned Chandigarh, but could not get in touch with you. Indiraji wanted to invite you to dinner."

I asked her if I could cash this rain cheque now.

"I'll try. Are you here for some days?"

I told her that I would be in the Capital for four days.

The third day a message came from Usha that Jeannie and I

were invited to the Prime Minister's House for an early supper at seven p.m.

I phoned Jeannie at Chandigarh to join me.

It was the 11th of December 1972. Jeannie spent all day polishing her nails, doing her hair, and got ready in the evening, wearing black leotards, a matching skirt, coat, and black gloves which she had bought in Paris.

I drove my open red car to the P.M.'s house.

It was foggy. When I reached the railway level crossing the gates were closed. Twenty minutes unnerved me. I reached 1, Safdarjang Road, ten minutes late.

I hurriedly parked the car outside when two tall men in lounge suits walked up to me, "Sir, you cannot park here. It's the Prime Minister's residence. Please park the car across the road. There !"

I mumbled, "Sorry. I've an appointment with the Prime Minister. I'm already late ... ten minutes ... it's ... I'm late."

Puzzled, they looked at me, checked my name and immediately said, "Please drive in." I jumped into the car. The guard flung open the gate and I drove in.

A whiff of roses invaded my nostrils. Roses in the dark ... their smell as thick as the fog.

Usha greeted us in the hallway and we were led to a tiny room. No decorations, except a large photograph of Pandit Nehru and a painting on the wall. A maroon carpet and three chairs in one corner with a low table.

All day I had been thinking of what to say to her. That afternoon walking in the Trade Fair grounds by the side of the sunlit lake, I had wondered at the power of this woman. She was at the crest of her popularity wave. After winning the Bangladesh war, she had emerged as the supreme leader.

A woman surrounded by mystery, she kept her distance

from everyone, yet warmed people's hearts with her flashing smile. Going over my thoughts I decided that I would not talk about my play.

While I sat musing, I heard a silken rustle. Indira Gandhi walked into the room.

She shook hands with Jeannie and asked her to be seated. There was silence for half a minute. It seemed an eternity.

Finally, I talked about the roses which had greeted us on the lawn with their fragrance. She said, "Well, my father loved roses. Our old gardener brought him a red rose every morning. His last offering to my father was a red rose."

Jeannie had long silken hair which looked like a burnished gold cascade. That morning she had read in the papers that a school teacher had been sacked for coming to school with her hair in a bob-cut.

She related this incident to Mrs. Gandhi and asked, "Is it not unjust, when the Prime Minister herself has bobbed hair?"

Mrs. Gandhi was not ready for such a question. Taken aback, she replied, "There is no such law for hair style. I have thick hair. It is difficult to manage it, wash it, treat it, comb it, fix it. It's time-consuming. To avoid wasting time, I trim it."

The white streak in her hair had become her hallmark, her signature. She must spend a lot of time grooming it. She was meticulous about the fold of her saree, its colour and texture. Also, the minutest detail of her hair setting.

The servant brought a tray and set it on the table. Lichi juice, sweets, sandwiches, dates.

She sipped lichi juice.

Jeannie had tasted American juices and squashes, but this drink had a strange flavour.

Mrs. Gandhi explained : "It's lichi, very refreshing and healthy ... *lee-chi* ... a Chinese fruit. We had trade with China in ancient times ... silks and brocades ... even fruit trees."

We ate our supper, rather nibbled at it gingerly.

"Today, I visited a photo-exhibition on Panditji's life and saw your childhood pictures." I said. "You had very large eyes ..."

She smiled, "Yes, embarrassingly large. Now they have become smaller."

She talked of eyes. "The Europeans have cold eyes ... green and blue ... smaller as compared to Indian eyes ... our eyes are warm, expressive, full of emotion ... our poets have composed thousands of songs on the beauty of the eyes."

Suddenly she said, "I saw your *Sultan Razia*. Were you satisfied with the production?"

"Yes, I was ... Alkazi added much visual power and emotion to it."

"He is very talented."

A few more remarks about Alkazi's directorial genius and then she asked me, "Why did you show Razia as a weak character? She couldn't have been weak. She ruled over powerful Turkish lords. She must have been a woman with a strong will."

Her grandson Rahul toddled in and clambered up her lap. Pulling at her sari *pallav*, he said, "*Daadi* ... come."

"Don't mind him. He is my pet." She patted him.

After a little while Rahul went out.

We continued talking for about half an hour.

Usha peeped in, Mrs. Gandhi got up, flashed a smile at us, said good-bye, and disappeared behind a raw silk curtain.

M arie Seaton, film historian, often visited India and camped in the homes of various high-ups. A compulsive talker, loaded with knowledge of artists, directors, film makers and celebrities, she sometimes stayed at Teen Murti as Panditji's guest. She would join Panditji at breakfast and freeze the table with her talkathons, or would appear in a crumpled saree draped miserably around her skeleton frame.

She often came to my house and sat in the courtyard correcting proofs of her book on Satyajit Ray, enjoying tea and talking endlessly. Her book on Eisenstein—an eye-witness account of film making by this great Russian master—had become a classic of film literature. She had gone with him to Mexico as his mistress and had made a short film piecing together leftover strips and half-finished shots.

Her knowledge of people, events, arts, sex, and details of her life were most absorbing, but became boring when continued too long.

One day she said, "I have lived as a guest in Panditji's house for months. Indira has looked after me very well. I'd like to repay her hospitality. I've arranged evening tea for her in a luxurious apartment in Golf Links. My friend who owns it has gone to Japan and has left it to me for a week. But it is proving very expensive. Indira likes *gobhi ka pakoras* ... I would like your cook to prepare *pakoras* and serve them sizzling hot. You are also invited."

Marie was abnormally tight-fisted. She had invited me as she needed my cook.

At the party were Habib Tanvir, Indrani Rehman, the hoary Kamala Devi Chattopadhyaya, two artists (I forget their names), Indira Gandhi, Marie and I. Indira sat casting languid looks at the people. I remember only her ivory face, long pale fingers and her smile. Marie talked all the time. After one hour of her gabble, the party was over.

After the Emergency in 1977, Indira Gandhi lost the elections. All calculations went wrong. The Janta wave brought Morarji Desai to power, a surly thin-lipped old man—puritanical, staunch, stubborn. The press bayed for Indira's blood. The Shah Commission was set up. The whole nation joined in baiting her. Loyalists changed sides. She was dazed.

I thought it would be interesting to meet her. I rang her up at her Wellington Crescent residence. I was given an appointment to meet her at 10 a.m.

On arrival I saw a desolate kothi. Its main gate was wide open. No cars and scooters. A weather-beaten screen of dried palm leaves shielded the front. It was a ravaged house.

Her Private Secretary, R.K. Dhawan, sat in a small tent with a few old men in khaddar caps dozing in their chairs. I gave him my card. Dhawan asked me to take my seat.

I had taken with me a pictorial booklet of the folk play *Mirza Sahiban* which had a folk motif on its cover. I borrowed a pen from Dhawan and inscribed "To Indiraji" and a line from Tagore's poem, "Is there music only in the rising waves, and not in the falling waves?"

Suddenly Dhawan said, "Come?" I hurriedly got up and followed him.

Mrs. Gandhi stood on a low platform outside the verandah. She wore sun glasses, a bunch of newspapers in the crook of her arm. A group of people stood at a lower level, beseeching her. I wondered from where these people had come. Perhaps they had sat behind the tent, somewhere in the bushes, waiting to see her. They looked peasants in dhotis, and turbans, and caps. They complained of high prices, floods and begged for her help.

She squinted her eyes, folded her hands, and said, "I'm no longer the Prime Minister. Go to them whom you have voted for. I can help no longer. Thank you for coming." The crowd melted.

She looked at me and said, "Let's go inside."

The room was cold and bare. She put her handbag and the bundle of newspapers on the sofa, took off her glasses and said, "Yes...?"

I sat puzzled. Why had I come to her? What did I want? Her stare froze me. I had come to see her on an impulse.

"Yes ...?"

I regained my breath and said, "Indiraji, people are discussing you everywhere. Tea sellers, dhabawallas, washermen, panwallas, clerks, artists, bankers. The Congress has lost. But people have a large emotional fund for you."

She kept silent. I did not know how to break the ice. She noticed the book in my hand. I presented it to her. She started thumbing its pages and read the lines "Is there music only in the rising waves ...?" She had been a student at Santiniketan ... might have chanted this very song.

She screwed up her eyebrows. "Do the present rulers understand poetry and culture? Do they understand Tagore? They talk about kisans without understanding their culture. They are after Sanjay's blood. They want to wipe out my family. Someone suggested that I should leave the country otherwise they will arrest me ... torture me ... I snubbed them. Why should I leave? I am a part of this soil ... its people. Do you know they have bugged my phones? Some families with whom we have had deep relations for generations are afraid to meet me. It's terrible ... Where have they gone? I never realised that people could change their loyalties overnight. It's not defeat which bothers me. In elections, victory and defeat are a part of the game. But my personal friends ... friends of my father ... people whom I had tied rakhi and who called me a sister and vowed life-long friendship ... they have gone. Whom should I trust? Perhaps there is no personal loyalty in politics ... I don't understand ... It hurts me ..."

Tears glimmered in her eyes. She was pouring out her heart to me like a desolate queen. Tagore's lines had triggered her pent-up emotions, filled her with anguish.

That was the last time I saw her.

13

An emotional storm raged in me during my stay in Chandigarh. This most precious time of my life was spent in rehearsals, productions, teaching, directing and working in the studio. Imprisoned in a cocoon, I tasted bliss, torture, passion—the noblest and darkest moments of my life.

For nine years I was in Panjab University as Head of the Theatre Department. Universities breathe a peculiar smell of old books, musty ideas, quotations, senate meetings—a smell as distinct as that of an aeroplane or a hospital. I had never wanted to be a member of the Senate or Academic Council. Typists typed the speeches of old professors who sat in meetings and spouted their moral and educational *'bak bak'*. The typists constantly punched iron keys, rattling words onto long sheets which were thrown into the dustbin every three months. The whole process reminded me of a mad house. After my term finished in 1977, I returned to Delhi. Jeannie and I had split. She was aching to return to Seattle. My nine-year-old son Manu and six-year-old daughter Jannat were the fruits of Chandigarh. We did not divide them like property but told them that they belonged to both of us.

When I landed in Delhi, I had 326 rupees in my pocket—my life's savings—plus an electric typewriter, a tea kettle, books, and a few odd possessions.

My neighbourhood was alive. Early morning voices of hawkers filled the air. Somewhere a trumpeter blew a resonant marching tune which floated above the hub-bub of the street. The familiar smells and sounds of the lane brought me back to my old world.

In my absence, the electricity had been disconnected for non-payment of dues and my house was dark. I sat in the courtyard in the reflected glow of the city lights which rose like golden smoke. For sometime I sat watching the sky through the champak leaves. Then I remembered that I had to finish a short article for a Punjabi magazine that very evening to meet the deadline.

I asked my servant to pull out a tall brass worship lamp from my theatre props and light it. He dug it out from the storeroom, cleaned it, filled it with coconut oil, lit its five fat wicks and put it on my table. I enjoyed working in the yellow light of its swaying flames, the smell of oil fumes reminding me of my village.

For three nights I read in the spluttering flames which cast eerie shadows on the walls and made my eyes water. I was accustomed to the amber light of shaded bulbs and could not stand this theatrical lamp. I decided to raise money to pay the bill.

I borrowed mostly from the hefty Tandon, owner of a motor garage who bossed over his two sons and twenty mechanics. He could repair a car of any make. He had a strong-lined face, a puckered forehead and a gruff voice—a man from the Frontier. He moved in his workshop like an old wolf, but his appearance belied his temperament. He was extremely gentle.

Addressing me in hyperboles, he would say, "An honour to serve you, my dear great writer. Noblest son of this earth! A precious gem. I am your servant. Ask me anything at dead of night, I'll provide."

I always approached him when I was at the end of my resources. He would arrange money in no time.

Another of my benefactors was the bushy-bearded electrician Maghar Singh, a drunk. Over the years he had become a lumbering wreck. He would go to any extent to extract money from people, saying his wife was seriously ill, or his children's school fees had not been paid, but he would blow it up on liquor.

I saw Maghar walking in the sun, bleary-eyed from a hangover.

I said, "Maghar, have you some money?"

Wiping his lips, he said, "Sir, as much as you want."

He untied his girdle, opened its folds and showed me a bundle of crisp currency notes. "Take fifty or hundred, as much as you need."

I explained my problem to him. "How can they cut your light?" He scratched his beard, reflected and said, "Don't worry. I know everybody in the Electricity Department. I'll get your connection restored."

I went with him to the musty building of the New Delhi

Municipal Corporation. Its corridors were dark, the walls spattered with pan spittle, burnt-out bidis and rubbish lying in the verandahs. Maghar Singh led me through the maze, up two flights of uneven steps, worn down by the constant stream of supplicants. We entered a poorly lit barrack filled with clerks, scribbling in their thick old registers and gossiping.

Maghar Singh stood before the head of the section, a bespectacled bald man with a drooping moustache. He introduced me, "Chopra Sahib! This is our great writer Balwant Gargi ... meet him ... a Padma Shri ... a great writer ... his electricity connection has been cut. He is known everywhere ... America, London, Russia ... Don't you know him?"

Chopra scowled, "What do you want Maghar? Are you drunk?"

Maghar folded his hands. "My request is that Gargi Saheb's electricity connection be restored. How can he write his stories without light? He cannot pay the bill now. He will pay in instalments ... please ... have mercy *badshaho* ..."

Chopra shouted for some Sharma and Sharma shouted for some Verma who was in charge of the defaulters. He checked the register and told me that I had to pay eleven hundred rupees plus another four hundred as security. He couldn't accept instalments. The payment had to be made in a lumpsum.

Maghar again begged that they should have some consideration for a great writer. But they were adamant. "No one can break the rules, not even Indira Gandhi," said Chopra.

He started scribbling in his register without looking up again. I was angry with Maghar. Why had he brought me to this place? I left the room. Maghar followed me like a whipped dog. On second thought I realised that he was only trying to help me by begging from table to table. I held him by the arm and dragged him out. Maghar scratched his beard, "They are dogs.

They want a bone. But before their superiors, they piss in their pants."

I decided to sell my imported tape-recorder, record player, and an old Sony two-in-one. I put these in my car and went to a Defence Colony shop whose owner knew me. He gave me Rs. 2000 for the lot. After paying the electricity bill, I had five hundred left in my pocket. I invited a friend to the Taj Hotel and we sat in the Machan, overlooking the swimming pool, enjoying coffee and banana-splits.

I came back and sat on my throne, a wooden divan. My *dhiansthal*, seat of concentration. Sitting in one place gave me power. I thought of Yogis and Buddha ... eternally still ... the Himalayas ... the stillness of a stone ... its atoms circling and clinging to each other. Did I know the mind of a stone? Did a stone think? Did it communicate to its partner... ? dream ... love ... weep ...?

I stared at the brass table lamp, the electric typewriter. They were silent. The black telephone sat like a depressed puppy. My eyes wandered to the cracked mud walls, the ceiling, the bookshelf, the Picasso, and back to myself. I looked at my hands. They were full of energy, mind clear, my body in tone.

14

Reshma, the gypsy singer from Pakistan, had invaded the Capital. Everyone was keen to see her and listen to her legendary voice.

I had heard her for the first time in 1968 when her recorded song *Hai o Rabba* was smuggled into India. A haunting voice. She was famous before she came here.

I invited her to my house for dinner.

She said, "People invite me and then ask me to sing. I don't like to sing just for their *wah wah*! Can I fill my belly with their *wah wah*? Or medals? Or scrolls? If I sell all these in the flea market, they wouldn't fetch me even one meal."

"This dinner is in your honour" I said "...to celebrate your visit ... to meet friends who are your fans. I promise I won't ask you to sing in my house."

She agreed.

At eight o'clock she came with her husband and son. She was tall and plump. In her baggy silk shalwar, loose flowing shirt and a gold-spangled green shawl, she looked overpowering. Her husband wore a Pakistani bottle-green shirt and shalwar, topped by an embroidered jacket.

I welcomed them as they hugged me twice, turn by turn, and ushered them into the room where 20 people were waiting for them: opera singer Madan Bala Sindhu, Sakhish Pandit, his wife Kusum, composer poet Sheila Bhatia, Uma Vasudev, Usha Bhagat and some actors, writers and friends. They got up and welcomed her. Reshma hugged and blessed everybody, invoking Allah and Hazrat Chishti.

She sat down on the padded quilt on the floor, chewing pan and tobacco and beaming at everybody. Particularly arresting were her eyes ... steel grey with a golden glint, like a desert animal's.

To entertain Reshma, Madan Bala Sindhu started singing a Punjabi folk song in her melodious voice. Reshma stared at her with her hypnotic eyes. Madan Bala's voice cracked. She began perspiring. She could hardly complete the song.

Reshma said, "I want to sing. Do you have a harmonium?"

"No."

"A drum?"

"No."

"What sort of artist are you? Allah! I always carry a drum and a harmonium and my husband and son with me. Then we are self-sufficient."

She sent her son in a taxi to bring the instruments from her hotel.

She regaled us with stories of her foreign trips. We laughed at her wit and malapropisms. She praised India's hospitality, but hastily switched to Pakistan's President, "Zia Saheb is our Badshah. He has a heart of gold. He gave me a ring set with turquoise ... this gold bracelet. He is the king of kings. May Allah bless our Zia Saheb! May Allah protect him from lightning and thunder!"

She was a mix of ignorance and cunning, and repeated stories of her life at every *mehfil*. People listened to these and laughed because she made them juicy by her mannerism. She said to me, "This shawl, woven in gold thread, was presented to me by the President of Urdu Conference. A rich man of Allah!"

But the organisers told me that Reshma had extracted this shawl by insisting that it was a 'must' for the opening ceremony. It had cost the organisers ten thousand rupees. She had also taken a large sum in cash, which she put in her purse.

Addressing herself in the third person, she said in a resounding voice,"Be grateful Reshma! Allah has blessed you with a voice. Allah's breath is in your throat. You sing at His command." Then reverting to the first person, she said, "Balwantji, what have I to do with titles? My name is enough. I sing free of charge at the tombs of Pirs. I go to Hazrat Aulia's *dargah* and make the offering of a *chaddar,* a cauldron of goat meat and saffron rice. Why should I sing in the houses of *amirs*. They must pay!"

Her husband and son returned with the harmonium and the drum.

She started with *Hai o Rabba* and her voice rose, full of yearnings, the physical incarnation of this legendary song which had united India and Pakistan across borders. She said, "There is no visa for my voice. My songs travel to India before I do."

She resumed her song, creating minarets and domes in space ... architectural forms, hypnotising us ...the song had echoes of

Lorca's heroines, gypsy fires leaping from her throat. We sat spellbound.

Then she said, "I'm hungry. I sing better when my stomach is full. I keep chunks of roast lamb beside me. When I sing, I like a bite."

We came out into the courtyard. A large cauldron of hot spiced meat curry, *biryani*, roast chicken, vegetables and *tandoori* chapattis. It was almost 11 o'clock when we finished our dinner. Reshma said, "Allah knows, I have not eaten such delicious meat in India. This seems to be cooked by a Muslim. I don't like meat cooked by Hindus, who can cook only *daal* and chapattis. I live in a tiny hotel as a guest of the great Nanda Sahib but I cook meat myself in my little kitchen."

By now the story of Reshma is well known. Her father, a *banjara*, belonged to Bikaner and traded in horses and camels. The caravan would sometimes cover fifty miles in one trek, moving from Bikaner to Bahawalpur. Once, the caravan travelled to Peshawar. Reshma was born there and grew up in gypsy camps.

"I used to sing walking on the sands," Reshma said. "My voice would rise high over the caravan bells. I did not learn from anyone. I don't know *ragas* and *raginis*. I have no training. Only Allah has taught me. His notes are in my throat, in my breath. I don't do any *riaz*. I can't imagine myself sitting in the corner of a little room practising. I sing in the open. The sky is my studio. I sing from the pit of my stomach. This voice rises from my navel and blows through my lungs and throat. Today's singers sing with their lips. There is no emotion in such songs. Films have ruined our music."

She laughed a deep gypsy-throated laughter.

Reshma's style is unusual. She squeezes the total power of the notes, extracting their blood. She cannot be compared to

Lata Mangeshkar or Begum Akhtar or Surinder Kaur, who are basically *mehfil* singers.

After dinner she sat in the courtyard on a wooden divan and asked her son to play the drum. Her husband started playing on the harmonium and Reshma started singing haunting melodies of the desert in her native tongue ... and continued till the wee hours of the morning.

It was a cold rainy night. The bell rang. The servant opened the door. I heard the sound of heavy footsteps and a booming voice. It was Reshma and her husband.

She hugged me and said, "We are gypsies ... forlorn ... just now coming from Jalandhar and Ludhiana ... that wretched Punjab of yours. No place to stay. We thought of you. You are a great man ... your heart is large like the sky. Allah has given you this heart. In Delhi we know many rich people who worship me and make me sing all night. They live in palaces, but will not house me. Their dogs sleep on velvet. But they don't care for an artist. May Allah bless you ...!"

I welcomed them and asked the servant to bring food for them. He rushed to a nearby Peshawari dhaba and brought chicken *biryani*, fried *daal* and oven-fresh chapattis, and served these with raw onions and green chillies. Reshma put her little bundle to one side, took off her shawl and sat down to eat, relishing each morsel.

She told me that she had gone to Punjab to sing in a *mehfil*. She sang without charging a paisa—just for the love of Punjab. But she was harassed by officials. A local newspaper wrote that she had charged twenty-five thousand rupees per recital. It was a lie! Reshma's face flushed with anger and she spoke in a high-pitched voice, "That horrible Hindu paper! that *lala*! May Allah send him to hell! Roast him in fire! That bastard! Son of a pig! Son of a *khanjir*! That mother-raper ...that infidel ... May Allah cut his throat and make his house barren! ... May his tongue rot ... May he be struck with leprosy ... That mother-fucker ...!"

She cursed the Hindu editor who was my friend. She forgot that I also was a Hindu.

A stream of filth flowed from that throat which poured out songs of beauty, love and yearnings ... melodies which haunted everybody. That throat had now turned into a sewer. A river of mud.

She slept on the straw-matted floor, her husband by her side, wrapped in heavy cotton quilts. I slept on my wooden divan.

At midnight, shuddering sounds awakened me. It was Reshma snoring.

She lay like a she-demon, one of those primeval characters celebrated in our folklore.

The Punjab government officer who had left her at my door met me the following day. He told me that the two societies in Jalandhar and Ludhiana had paid Reshma in cash. Stamped receipts were required for the auditors. She created a scene, saying that she was not allowed to sing for money in India. She would be whipped if Zia Saheb came to know of it. Her husband reluctantly signed the receipts in a crazy scrawl.

The news had leaked to a local newspaper which praised Reshma's voice as a cultural bridge between the two Punjabs, but also mentioned that she was paid Rs. 25,000 in cash for each session. This had infuriated Reshma.

Why was she telling lies?

I had known of sadhus who had renounced wordly possessions fighting over a loaf of bread; of revolutionaries jailed for patriotism stealing a cigarette from their comrades; a great dancer who quarelled over a petty payment to her drummer.

Perhaps there is some deep relationship between greatness and pettiness. The two co-exist in one person—the two opposite forces responsible for greatness.

15

One afternoon the phone rang. It was Parveen Babi calling from Bombay. "Balwantji, I am coming to Delhi tomorrow and shall be staying at the Maurya Sheraton. I'll have dinner with you and Khushwant Singh. Decide between the two of you—where?"

I was surprised. The most beautiful and seductive actress of the Bombay film world! She lived alone in her bachelor apartment and had had a series of sensational love affairs. She had never learned to act but was sought after by producers for her glamour. At the peak of her career she had suddenly disappeared leaving behind many films unfinished, ruining the producers. Later, people learnt that she was washing dishes in a New York restaurant. After two years, healed of her wild and crazy actions, she returned to Bombay. The film industry embraced her and she became a star once again.

I first met her in 1981 at a party at Sanjay Khan's—the flamboyant film producer-actor-director. As she walked in, a warm wave ran through the party. She smiled and shook hands with everyone. She told me that she had read my novel and invited me over for a cup of coffee to her apartment.

When I went to see her, she was in her nightie, her long black hair tousled. She sat on a cushion placed over a straw mat and lighted a cigarette. During the conversation on art, literature, films, I asked her way she had disappeared. "I was ill ... a different kind of illness," she said. "I couldn't help my actions. I tried to control myself but a surging wave overtook me. Another force, another being, with a superior will. I was in the grip of that superior being, my Double ... a superior Parveen Babi who commanded me. But now I'm all right. I love to work in films. I am grateful to my producers. Why don't you come to my shooting tomorrow?"

The next day I watched her on the sets of a dance-action film. She wore shiny knee-high leather boots, black shorts with a silver and gold fringe, and black leather boots, a jacket studded with metal buttons and chains.

After the shot, she joined me at a special table where lunch was laid for us. In the midst of the meal she suddenly got up and walked over to a weasely old man with a spongy nose. He was wearing a dhoti and a thin white cotton kurta under a sleeveless jacket. She greeted him, and began pleading with him, but he was not agreeing to her request. I could not hear what she was saying. Was he a money lender? Or a builder ...?

Maybe she owed him money ... a six figure instalment. I wondered why she was begging. Millions of her fans were ready to be at her feet. ... worshipping her ... eager to have a glimpse of her. She put her hand on his shoulder, trying to melt him, but he waved a "No" to her and walked away. Her face fell and she returned.

"What was the matter?" I asked

"This old man is a retired film editor. His son died last year. Now he is a lost soul. He has no interest in life, and wants to commit suicide. I was arguing with him that life is precious ... he must live. Enjoy life. But he is depressed ... I cannot bear it. I wanted to kiss him. I want to give him joy. "

Now after one year she had called from Bombay. I was thrilled. I rang up Khushwant and fixed up dinner at his house. I drove my convertible with its top down and reached the Maurya at 7.30 to pick up Parveen, cursing myself for being late. She was strolling in the foyer in a black silk maxi, silk stockings and high heeled sandals. Her hair, smoothly brushed, fell to her hips. She turned, swinging her hair, greeted me and got into my car.

I took a short cut and passed through a deserted road. Icy winds from the Himalayas were sweeping down to the plains. Parveen was feeling cold ... street lamps glimmered in the fog. Suddenly a thought crossed my mind : I was carrying a million-dollar star in my car ... the most precious and beautiful woman ... some bandit might hold us at gun point and rape her! I was foolish to have taken this route.

When I reached Khushwant's apartment, he opened the door and shot at me. "Shame on you, Balwant! You have robbed me of half-an-hour of Parveen's company." He hugged her and swept her into the room, where a dozen people were sipping Scotch and smoking.

He announced, "Meet Parveen Babi. She had once

declared that I was the man she loved most. I could not sleep for two nights out of sheer joy. Come Parveen. You are shivering." He handed her a hot punch and me a Scotch, and hurriedly introduced us to the party. "Meet John F. Kennedy. He is the son of the late President Kennedy." A slim young man in crumpled jeans sat with his American girl friend on a sofa, sipping *nimboo paani*. He got up and shook hands with us.

Khushwant settled down in a cushioned chair, covered his knees with a woollen shawl and balanced his legs on a round straw settee which he constantly rolled back and forth under his feet. On the side table rested an imported olive green telephone and an expensive gold fountain pen which he seldom used lest he should lose it. A back-lighted Buddha statue and a sword in a niche adorned his living room.

Son of a billionaire father who built New Delhi, Khushwant is the most shabbily dressed rich man I have seen—crumpled baggy Pathan trousers, unbuttoned khaddar shirt and a skimpy yellow turban. Like his father he has a strong jaw, a broad face and a well-groomed shiny beard, a twinkle in his eyes. He chews loaded betel leaves which have stained his once shining white teeth. But the sparkle of his laughter has not dimmed.

"What's John doing in India?" Parveen asked. "Is he interested in politics?"

"Which Kennedy can remain out of politics?" Khushwant replied. "He has inherited politics as well as wealth. They go together."

"Not in America," said John.

"There also they go together. The difference is that in America you have to be rich to get into politics. In India you get into politics to become rich!"

Mohanjeet Grewal, whom we called Minto, was also in

the party. Heavily perfumed, her eyes lined with collyrium, she was a sixty-year-old virgin, oozing energy. A tennis champion in her youth, she had gone to Europe in her twenties, and from there to New York where she fluttered in high society and had her picture in *Vogue*. She then moved to Paris to become a fashion designer, but ended up becoming a garment exporter.

She turned to John. "I used to know your mother many years ago."

"Really?" John looked at Minto, surprised, "I have never met you."

Minto smiled. "You were a kid at that time. I came to cover the tour of your mother in India and travelled all over with her."

John nodded and stirred his glass thoughtfully ... perhaps he was thinking of thirty years ago .. of his father ... and the days when his mother moved in the world as a queen of fashion.

"My mother now takes photographs and is writing for some magazines," John said. "Perhaps she will write her memoirs. That's the best thing the celebrities can do. She is still in the news."

We discussed how the media builds up images ... celebrities who earn millions by writing their memoirs. Stalin's daughter was paid half-a-million dollars by *Life* just for writing an article on her father.

"I want to earn money," Minto said suddenly. "Tons of money. I knew a Punjabi businessman in New York who earned millions. He had swanky cars, dogs, country villas, swimming pools. He bought an aeroplane. But then he realised so many millionaires had aeroplanes. He bought a stable, horses of rare pedigrees ... won the Derby ... but his lust for money would not end. He went into racing and gambling .. flew to Las Vegas casinos .. and lost everything. He ended up in a jail in India. But he had magic in his hands. Somehow, he managed to come out on bail, raised 800 million dollars and flew back to New York to pay off his debts and earn. I also have the same temperament. I want to earn ..."

"Why?"

"As a child I was brought up in luxury and have always maintained an expensive life style. With today's prices, I don't know ... I must save for my old days."

Parveen lit a cigarette, inhaled, and blew a cloud of smoke. "I do not want to save money. Or life. Some people never spend it. They hoard it. You can't put life in a bank locker and live on its interest. I want to burn the candle at both the ends."

Minto sighed, "I want to be happy. Just happy in my life."

A cardiologist laughed, "Happy? Happy? What a foolish idea! Happiness is not the purpose of life. A parrot is very happy. Evolution would have stopped at the parrot. But it continued and evolved the human mind ... eternally in anguish. What's the purpose of life?"

People looked at each other. The cardiologist continued, "When Freud was on his death bed in London, his 64-year-old disciple, a physician, asked him the same question. Freud reflected, closed his eyes, and said, 'The sole purpose of life is ...DEATH.'"

Parveen turned her eyes to Khushwant, "What type of death would you like?"

"A death without pain. I shouldn't know when it comes ...maybe I am writing ... or playing tennis ... or with my cats ... or making love. I am made of very strong bones. My uncle was ninety when he died. My father died when he was older than my uncle. I have lasted all these years and I'll last easily another twenty."

Minto sighed, "I want to die in my country. Death in New York or Paris is a curse. I believe in the ancient idea of dust mingling with dust, ashes to ashes, and becoming a part of the same earth. It's mystical but true. I would like to die in India."

Khushwant chuckled, "Anyone who was allotted a seat next to me in Parliament died. First it was the film star Nargis. A Hindi poet replaced her. He also died. Then Vishwanath Tiwari, a pompous poet-politician, a tough Punjabi, occupied the chair. He was shot dead a few months after that! May be it is now my turn to pop off. Death hovers on those seats."

After their imaginary obituaries, they resumed their drinks. The conversation turned to politics.

"India is sinking deeper and deeper into a bog," said Parveen.

"Who are doomed!"

"This country is a country of crooks."

"Corruption, greed, hate ... a country which boasts of the largest number of love songs is seething with hate."

"Churchill's prophecy is proving right. He had said that when the British quit, bastards and thugs will rule India. Now you see. Everywhere corruption. Bribes. Smuggling."

"Even birds have become smugglers", someone remarked. "A drug baron trained pigeons to fly from Peshawar to England, strapped tiny packets of heroin around the belly of each pigeon and set the flock off. They stopped on islands along the way—their rest rooms—and alighted on a house in a London suburb. Who could suspect these innocent birds?"

"Smuggling is an art. It needs imagination. Do you know the latest? A child holding an X-mas doll was walking with his mother through the customs. The doll fell from his hand and it spilled pearls. The mother was arrested."

Arguments and counter-arguments dissolved into fresh

topics.

A lanky journalist remarked, "Our politicians are sex hungry. The great Radhakrishnan was one. While he was reading Upanishads and analysing Vedas, his roving eye would sparkle at the sight of a woman. He had many affairs."

"How can you say that?"

"His son Gopal has talked about it. It makes Radhakrishnan more human. A philosopher who revelled in sex. He was a yogi and a bhogi."

"Sex is the greatest force. Depends how you use it. Picasso ... Modigliani, Toulouse-Lautrec painted nudes ... women drunk with sex. Amrita Sher-Gil looked at her naked image in the mirror and painted her beautiful nudes...."

"Dinner is ready!" Kaval, Khushwant's wife, announced.

Khushwant said, "Wait, Parveen hasn't finished her second drink."

"Let her carry it to the table," Kaval said sternly.

My first glimpse of Kaval had been in Lahore while she was playing tennis in a spotless white *shalwar-kameez*, a muslin *chunni* strapped diagonally across her chest. Sharp-featured, tall, with a complexion like beaten gold, she was a high-profile beauty. She had aged gracefully—a pale, lined face, and steel-grey hair. A formidable presence.

We all lined up for dinner, cooked by their hereditary servants.

After dinner, Kaval served pan. Khushwant explained to John, "It's a fragrant green leaf. We apply slaked lime and brick-brown *kattha* and top it up with nuts, cardamom and spices. We chew it until it dissolves in the mouth. You must have seen our street walls splattered with blood. Even our Parliament House walls... it's actually betel juice which the habituals spit out. It causes all sorts of cancers—throat cancer, tongue cancer, palate cancer ..."

"And you still chew it?" John asked.

"Like cigarettes. There is a publicity campaign against smoking. Yet millions smoke."

"It's nearing nine!" Kaval broke in. "Time for Khushwant to retire. So, good night!"

Parveen was a late-night person. Her parties generally started at ten and lasted till four.

As Kaval herded us out, Khushwant followed us barefoot to the large forecourt. Holding Parveen's hand, he said, "We'll meet again", and vanished into his apartment.

We stood outside wondering what to do. The night was young and cold. Parveen did not know where to go!

16

It had been raining all day. I was running a slight temperature and felt depressed. My documentary on Satish Gujral was half-finished. A novel and two plays were also half nibbled. Everything was at a loose end. A strange uneasiness was in my mind.

I had known Satish for the last thirty years and watched his art grow to formidable proportions—from painting to murals to architecture. His black fringed beard had turned grizzly grey, matching his thick mop of hair. His burning eyes were the most prominent feature on his face.

I had done some shooting of my film on him—his paintings, family, studio, environment, and shown him sketching and working. He was not much inspired by my approach. At times he would sit silent, disinterested, pre-occupied, and bored. One day during the shooting, he suddenly turned to me, "I must be frank with you. Your approach is most mechanical. I am not involved in it. I am doing what you are telling me to do in these strong lights, moving about, drawing, painting, but all this looks fake. I am not an actor. I can't paint on command, hold my brush and attack the canvas ... or change my mood from this to that. It's all very silly. Better we stop the film here and let me go over my own thoughts. Let me see the rushes of what has been filmed so far."

I refused to show him the rushes and explained, why. "The creation of a documentary film is like painting. You cannot predetermine every stroke of colour. Sometimes the artist himself does not know if he is going to apply vermilion or turquoise or a sudden sweep of chalk-white. He is working with a vague visualisation and continues to explore the miracle of colours and forms with a loaded brush, attacking the canvas by impulses. Film making is like that. After shooting, the film is worked on at the editing table with the available material, and by refrains of colours, transfers, intercuts and surprise juxtapositions of images, the director creates the required rhythm. Only at the editing table would I know exactly what I have done."

He protested, "No, I must be involved in the creative process. Even when my fractured leg was being operated on, chunks of flesh and bone paste were taken from my right hip to be fixed in my left thigh, I was watching the operation. How can I be a medium in a film without knowing what's happening? I want to watch myself in it and cannot be just a blind and automatic instrument, not knowing what's being filmed. From which angle? In what light? What composition? What colours and rhythms and textures? I want to know how you have taken the shot of my oil paintings. Have you followed the brush strokes, the sweep of my hand? Or taken long shots and close-ups according to the cameraman's viewpoint? It's very important for me to watch the work."

Satish stuck to his argument. The shooting was postponed, and I waited for him to be in right mood.

Kiran, Satish's wife, phoned me to come over and discuss the shooting schedule.

When I entered his room I saw him lying in bed, his head propped up by a heavy pillow, his legs stretched out at two different angles. He beamed. "Where have you been? Here I lie like a modern painting, my two legs like the two noses of a Picasso woman."

He had slipped and fallen from the parapet of a building he had designed which was under construction, and broken his left leg. Top orthopaedic surgeons in India had operated on his leg three times; the bones had been reassembled and refixed and he was advised to take complete bed rest. But he was restless, seething with energy. Now he was working on his latest project, the Belgian Embassy. He would travel in a palanquin down to his car and be driven to the site, where hobbling on his crutches, he would supervise the placement of every brick, tile, glass panel and door knob. He had not put any mural in the building because he had conceived it as a piece of multi-dimensional sculpture. Its turrets, arches, sliced domes and landscaped surroundings seemed to grow out of the earth.

Kiran fixed a drink for me, and we started talking about the film.

"The Films Division people are very unhappy with me", I said. "I dare not go to their office. The film has been delayed for almost two years now."

"I'll go with you to the office and meet the chief," Satish said with gushing energy. "How can they hurry through the film? Who gives them power over my life and death? I'll talk to them. Relax. You have a temperature. It will soon come down. Don't worry, we'll finish the documentary. I am involved in it. Whenever I discuss a film it is always in terms of the visual. You know, I do not hear words, nor sounds, nor music. I see only pictures, their visual power and movement. I find this supreme in Satyajit Ray. If his films have moved me to the depths of my soul, it is all through their visuals. In a way it is an advantage because I concentrate on the form, on the frame, on the composition, on the colour, textures and movement."

He had been lying in bed for seven months. I wondered how he could lie patiently and cheerfully for such a long period. Kiran had advised him to read and occupy his mind with some diversion. "I cannot read all the time because my own mind is set on a course of creation," said Satish. "I am involved in designing all the time, even when I am not actually doing so. A full work of sculpture is already forming in my mind. As soon as I am able to sit up it will be ready ... Every accident is minor ... nothing is significant, except death — the greatest accident. After the operation, I looked at my thigh crisscrossed from surgery, but I did not lose heart, because my mind is intact. I have the strongest defence against death. Because I can create. Frustration will come only when I cease to create."

On his bed lay scattered *Time, Newsweek* and *India Today*. He had devoured all the news. We gossiped about Bombay artists, models, and international trade fairs where hundreds of artists had been commissioned to create murals, friezes, and sculptures, their work to last for only a fortnight in view. After that the whole art treasure was scraped off.

"Murals have become mere decorations in paint ... like bunting and flags ... only to create colour noise," said Satish. "The painters know it and the authorities know it, and this whole colour riot goes on. It's good in a way. Better than mere bricks and concrete. At least the artists are clothing cold steel and cement. Murals were created by masters to have a lasting visual message of beauty and power ... Now they are like plastic toys. Well ..."

Kiran's face was drawn. She seemed to be pre-occupied. "You look worried," I said. "What's the matter?"

Looking at Satish, she said, "His leg is not healing. It has stood four operations. The doctors tell me that it has to be amputated."

"But I can see the muscle movement of his foot and leg, and it looks as if everything is alright."

"No," she said. "It has been going on for the last two years. The best bone-specialists in the world have been consulted. Top surgeons. One American specialist who is being considered for the Nobel Prize. But I am told that his leg will be cut below the thigh."

A tremor ran through her face. Tears welled up in her eyes, and she started sobbing.

Satish held her hand. "Don't worry, my dear. Don't cry for my leg. It's nothing. It is merely an accessory. What I need are only three things : my mind in perfect tone, my hand to execute the work directed by my mind, and my eyes. My inspiration comes from my guru Orozco. He lost his right arm, but he trained his left hand to draw and paint, and made world-famous murals of stunning beauty and power. Van Gogh led a colourless life but gave burning colours to the world. Toulouse-Lautrec, with his crippled short legs, walked with a stick to the brothels and cafes of Paris, and painted whores and dancing girls."

He took a deep breath and a gentle smile spread across his face. He turned to me and said, "Look at me. I am deaf. But does that matter? In many ways it has proved a boon. I have developed my vision, the power of seeing, observing, in a more intense way. I listen through my eyes. Above my neck there is nothing but one large eye. No ears, no nose. Just one burning eye, the eye of Shiva. It transforms every sense of smell or taste or sensation into a form. Into a design. You do not see the form as I do. When you speak of a table lamp, a telephone, a wine cup, you only hear these words and they give you a functional conception. When a cup passes before your eyes you still do not see it as a form, you see it as a function. You intellectualise it. You transform it into the idea. You do not see what I see."

In the grip of passion, he continued, "I was nine when I fell ill and lost my hearing power. In my childhood I suffered the ridicule of people for years. It depressed me. The social ridicule of a deaf man is far greater than that of a blind man. If you offer a cup of tea to a blind man he will extend his hand and grope for it, but you will not laugh at him. Rather you will help him. But if you speak to a deaf man and you say Gandhi and he hears it as *mandi* or *randi,* you will laugh. If he does not hear after two three times, you will be angry and ridicule him. But I overcame this shame because I had creative power. What are other people to me? What does it matter if I cannot hear their garbage. They are nobody. I am my own master."

I wondered how he would feel if he suddenly regained his power of hearing. I asked him, "Wouldn't it be great if you could hear ... listen to music, song, speech ...?"

He lip-read my words and propped himself up on his elbows. "Let me explain," he said with a shine in his eyes, "I see a table lamp shedding light. It communicates to me through light waves. Suppose the table lamp were to start talking, I would be shocked. The previous truth of the table lamp would disappear."

"When you see a man laughing, doesn't his face look like a mask to you?"

"Not really. When you laugh I hear a sound in my own way. Not literally, but I have an idea. Some people I link with a heavy voice, some with a tender voice. With every image I have linked a sound. This sound is my image of the sound. I am reconciled to it. I have developed my own meaning for every image. It has been so long that if tomorrow I were to start hearing, there would be a medley of new images. Utter confusion. Uma Vasudev might then be talking in the voice of my aunt, my wife in the voice of a laundress, and so on ..." He laughed.

The room was filled with energy. Everything was charged. We fixed the schedule of the film shooting and I came out of his villa-studio.

The roads glistened under the streetlights.

17

Dinner with Khushwant means seven o'clock. Like Moscow theatres whose publicity posters never mention the time of the show; everyone knows it is at seven.

Khushwant arrived with Kaval three minutes before schedule. Walking into my room, Kaval announced, "Fix me a double large Scotch with lots of ice!" and settled on a quilted rug in a corner to enjoy her Patiala peg.

Khushwant sat like Raja Indra, waiting to hold his durbar.

Sadia Dehlvi was the first to arrive. She stepped forward and planted a kiss on my cheek, leaving behind a red smudge and a whiff of fragrance. Her beautifully elongated eyes were right out of a Rajput painting.

Sadia had recently married the sixty-two year old

Jamaluddin, a high-profile executive of a multinational company in Islamabad. She had set a condition in her *nikah nama* that she would spend six months in India and six months in Pakistan, and retain her Indian nationality. In Pakistan, she had hit the headlines and appeared on Pakistan TV. Soon she became a darling of their high society, a much sought-after glamour woman.

"How is your old man?" Khushwant asked.

"I'm always attracted to older men," she laughed. "The story of my life is from one dirty old man to another. It's older men who have the finesse, the style and money to woo us. Like wine, they mature. They know the art of loving. I like men with a past!"

Close on her heels came Anita Singh who belonged to the princely house of Kapurthala. Her father, Raja Padamjit Singh, was a connoisseur of classical music. When he died, the divorcee princess moved to Delhi with music tingling in her royal veins. She was cheerful, bright-eyed and bejewelled, a glossy jet-black coif crowning her head.

When everyone was settled with their drinks, Anita leaned over and said, "You know where I went today. God! I went to G.B. Road! I never imagined in my life that I would ever visit that locality." She blushed.

G.B. Road was a haunt of prostitutes, a row of three-storey flats outside Ajmeri Gate, above shops of cement, marble and sanitary ware. It faced a big railway yard where engines shunted, and the constant roar of steaming, hissing and rattling of trains was heard. This was the place described by the Urdu writer Saadat Hasan Manto in his short story *The Black Shalwar* so brilliantly that people went to see the brothels as tourists visit Sherlock Holmes' Baker Street.

Anita was building a house in a posh locality where she could entertain friends and hold *mehfils*. She had gone to G.B.

Road to buy marble.

Uma Vasudev fluttered her eyelashes, "I'd love to visit these brothels. How sad that the singing girls have gone away from these *kothas*."

"But that's not true!" Anita protested. "That area is still full of whores and pimps."

Sixty years ago prostitutes and courtesans had lived in the heart of old Delhi, in Chawri Bazar. They had occupied the upper floors while the ground floors were shops of silks, jewellery and worship lamps. The shopkeepers protested that the prostitutes were sitting over their heads, singing lewd songs, soliciting customers, and selling their bodies. How could these whores remain in the heart of the city, polluting social and family life? There was a big agitation against them and they were thrown out from the locality. They moved with their *sarangiwallas, tabalchis* and paraphernalia, and settled outside Ajmeri Gate in a row of shop-cum-flats facing the railway yard.

Here they started afresh. Again this place became a flourishing business centre. And again there was an agitation against them. The Immoral Traffic Act 1956 was passed; prostitution was banned. But the prostitutes, posing as professional entertainers, practised their hereditary art of dance and music, and continued their trade. Occasionally some social crusader would raise a storm against prostitution, but then it would subside and the prostitutes carried on as before.

Recently prostitutes had taken out a procession in Delhi shouting the slogan, "We want our right to vote! Our birthright to carry on our profession with dignity!" It was led by Nimmo, an educated prostitute, who mobilised whores and pimps, and fought the general election for Parliament. She lost, but made her point.

Renuka, a firebrand feminist who had recently returned

from Europe after attending the World Conference on women's rights, said to Khushwant, "We are fighting to abolish prostitution. Why don't you help us in this noble cause?"

Khushwant replied, "I've never been to a prostitute's *kotha*. I have no experience in this field."

"But you have written a big article about prostitutes. You must help remove this social evil. Any man who buys a woman's body should be jailed."

Khushwant laughed, "I've never spent a penny on such a luxury. I enjoy free trips to Europe, free dinners, free drinks and free hospitality. I cannot speak about prostitutes."

Renuka's face flushed. "Men have made woman a sex doll. A thing to be sold in bazaars. Needy women, forced by economic compulsions, sell their body. That must be stopped."

I said, "In the fifties, the British outlawed prostitution, and all the streetwalkers immediately settled into apartments, which became brothels. In India, when the Government passed an Act against prostitution, the reverse happened : the *kotha* girls were driven from the brothels onto the street to become streetwalkers. You can't ban prostitution by passing laws. All that changes is form in which it is being carried on."

A Swedish woman, who was sipping Scotch in slow gulps and listening quietly, trying to understand the problem of dancing girls and prostitutes, said, "We have no prostitution in Sweden."

Uma pounced, "How come?"

"Because women of the upper class have entered the trade and driven out prostitutes."

"Delhi too is catching up," said Khushwant. "Who are these women? A man normally sleeps with twenty to thirty women in his lifetime. These women are not prostitutes, nor whores. They are the wives and sisters of people you might be knowing. These women pass as faithful and pure. Happy is the husband who does not know about his wife's faithlessness!"

He laughed with a twinkle in his eyes. He was chewing a betel leaf. His lips were red and wet, charged with the juices of the betel and the topic of prostitutes. "I've just returned from Germany, the richest and most flourishing country in the world. In their beautiful city of Hamburg I saw the largest number of prostitutes. There must be psychological and sociological reasons for this. Many women must be thinking why pound at the typewriter all day for a measly salary. Why not earn a hundred bucks for a few minutes in bed?"

I said, "I was directing the Sanskrit classic *The Prostitute and the Yogi* in New York. I asked the girls about the different types of prostitutes. They counted : harlot ... prostitute ... hooker ... tart ... slut ... street-walker ... broad ... strumpet ... whore. Every girl wanted to play the role."

"Why?"

"Perhaps every virtuous woman hides a whore in her."

The women howled. "How disgusting! You have a sick mind."

In the midst of heated conversations and fumes the cook had quietly arranged metal pots steaming with chicken curry, rice, spiced *daal* and *parathas* on the slim black table that served as my writing desk as well as dining table.

Everyone joined in dinner.

It was nearing nine. Time for Khushwant to leave. Kaval marched him out, carrying a package of left-over bones for her cats.

18

I saw Subhadra Butalia, wife of my college days friend, walking towards me at the India International Centre. She was a crusader for women, especially those ill-treated by their menfolk. I often joked about her feminist zeal. She said, "Enjoying coffee? Always coffee! You know she has gone?"

"Who?"

"Indira Gandhi."

"Where?"

Subhadra looked at me, her face drawn, "She is no more. Her own bodyguards pumped bullets into her. She has been taken to hospital. BBC says she is dead, but AIR is announcing that she is being operated upon by doctors. I think she is dead. Horrible!"

I was stunned. It confirmed the prophecy of Maghar

Singh. He had said that Indira Gandhi had signed her own death warrant the day she had ordered the Akal Takht to be fired upon. Nobody could protect her from this death.

The killers, her trusted bodyguards, had walked behind like shadows with sten guns and revolvers. In the act of protecting her, they became her killers. It reminded me of the story of the mythological Prince Parikshat who was prophesied to die by snakebite. His father, King Janamjay, performed a *sarpa* yagna which attracted all the snakes of three worlds to the flaming *havan kund,* in which they perished. A gardener brought a flower garland as an offering and put it around the prince's neck. A snake hiding in the garland bit the prince, who died instantly.

The murder of Indira Gandhi had the same irony. Its planning could not have been visualised by even the most imaginative story-teller. Two loyal Sikhs turned disloyal. They were loyal to Indira Gandhi, but after her Black Commandos had attacked the holiest of their holy shrines and desecrated the Golden Temple, their loyalty had changed.

They dipped their hands in the saffron water, drank *amrit* (nectar) and vowed to avenge the insult. They alone could kill her. Villains in the eyes of the establishment, they became martyrs for their community. Sweets were distributed in Patiala and Delhi. There was rejoicing in gurdwaras and *sangats.* As Indira Gandhi was shot and collapsed into a pool of her own blood on the lawns of her residence, she stared at the bearded guards, her last look fixed on them, and said, *"Kya kar rahay ho* (What are you doing)?"

Men wept, women wailed as they went around her repaired body lying in State.

Rioting broke out that night in the Capital and many other parts of the country. Looting, burning and killing of Sikhs started. It was said that Sikhs were being "taught a lesson" for killing the lady Prime Minister of India.

There was a loud thumping at my door. A raucous voice rang out, "Open the door! Open the door! Gargi Saheb, open the door!"

Whose was this strange voice? Again a loud thumping.

I opened the door. It was Maghar Singh, turban in hand and hair dishevelled. He rushed in and sank into a chair in the courtyard. "Give me the scissors! Quick! Blood is flowing ... Scissors!"

I went into the room to search for the scissors.

He grabbed the scissors from my hand and started clipping his beard and hair in quick snips. His long hair fell on the ground. In place of the beard was a patchy stubble. He looked ghastly.

He was shivering. "Give me a drink."

"I have no alcohol. Do you want tea?"

"Tea? I do not drink tea! Only wine ... Killing of Sikhs going on. My beard is Guru's harvest. It will grow again."

His gold-filled teeth shone in his ravaged face. His eyes were haunted. He gave me a look of tremendous sadness, and left.

Tara Singh phoned, his voice quaking, "Gargiji, in my *mohalla* they are looting and killing Sikhs. These are not Hindus of our neighbourhood, but people imported from villages, carrying spiked *lathis* and spears. Our house is not safe."

"Take a taxi and come here at once!"

"We are surrounded ..." The phone went dead.

What would happen to him? He lived across the Yamuna bridge in a Hindu majority colony. I started thinking of the killings during Partition. With these killings, there would be retaliation in Punjab. A fratricidal war.

I was in turmoil when the bell rang. The servant opened the door. Tara Singh and his three daughters came in. I hugged them, "Come in! You are safe here."

Tara Singh said, "I am completely shaken, Balwantji. I have braved poverty, illness, betrayal. Even murder. But this mass killing of Sikhs ... it's horrible. I am shaken."

He became quiet. His face had a bluish tinge ... a shadow of death. His daughters sat like frightened kittens. Then he said, "My brother-in-law's friend came in a taxi to rescue us. He is clean-shaven and looks like a Hindu. He called out and forced us into the taxi. But my wife wouldn't leave the house. She was worried about the TV set and the VCR. She wanted to bring these with her in the taxi. I threw them out and said, 'Save your life! Come!' But she clung to the TV set. The driver started the taxi and raced through the lane. My wife is left behind."

Tara Singh stood up, "I must go back and bring her."

"Are you mad? Your house is in the thick of rioting. You can't go."

I telephoned a few friends in the police and the press, but nobody could help. Tara Singh said, "I can't suffer the torture of being here while my wife is alone in that house."

"Don't be foolish. I won't let you go."

Tara Singh's face turned purple and his small eyes burnt behind the glasses. "I'm going to get my wife."

The daughters shrieked, "Papa, don't go! They will kill you!"

Tara Singh glared, "Don't squeal like pigs. I can't sit here. Eat the *halwa* Gargi has prepared; consider it *karah-prasad*. Chant the name of the Guru. I'll return."

He rushed out.

I did not know what to do. I had never seen Tara Singh so desperate, angry or irrational. Now his actions were fraught with danger. He had once told me, "Avoid the mob. It's a blind beast. It may attack the very people who are leading it."

Now he had jumped into the pit of fire. Was he seeking death?

An hour later I heard a vehicle halt outside the lane. Tara Singh emerged from a military jeep, helping his wife. With them was Gulzar Singh. He said loudly, "I went with Tara Singh for the sake of my *bhabi*. Here she is."

The three of them walked into the courtyard. The daughters ran to their mother sobbing and hugged her. Tara Singh said, "Where is your promised *halwa*? By the blessing of the Guru, we are back."

They settled down in the room. "You know? When I left here the roads were empty. I walked alone. A Sikh walking in a desert of silence ... my footsteps frightened me. I went to Gulzar's house. He had a friend, a Colonel, who lent his jeep to us. We roared across the Yamuna bridge to my house. I found my wife alone in her room, sitting beside the TV set. We picked up the TV and drove here. But I tell you, it was not the TV. My wife had hidden some gold ornaments in the mud wall. She had collected these during the last thirty years of our married life ... skimping, stealing from my pockets, and turned the savings into ornaments for the weddings of our daughters. My wife hid her treasure in a yellow silk handkerchief and tied it around her breasts. She sat in the house with her 'gold breasts'. I said to her 'Foolish woman! If someone grabbed you by the breasts, I would have lost you and the gold."

We laughed.

Gulzar rolled his eyes, "Bhabi is wiser than you!"

Tara Singh and his family hugged me and went in

Gulzar's jeep to his house, which had three bedrooms and was in a safe locality.

Cooped up in my room, I felt vague rumblings and came out into the courtyard. The sky was overcast with reddish smoke. I ventured out. All the shops were closed. There was nobody in the street. Not even a dog at the garbage dump. Only distant yells and rumblings.

I walked through Connaught Lane to Janpath to Regal Building. It seemed as if an army had marched through the streets, trampling out life.

I saw men armed with iron rods and steel-tipped *lathis* attacking shops owned by Sikhs, smashing showcases, looting and burning. It was methodically crazy. A man carrying a kerosene canister doused a shop and another flung a flaming torch. The shop burst into flames to shouts of *'Indira Gandhi amar rahay!'*

The mob attacked a musical instruments shop owned by a Sikh. They smashed glass cases and pulled out guitars, flutes, drums, harmoniums and violins. One zealous rioter grabbed a Gibson guitar to take it home. His colleague did not let him. They fought over it. He smashed it on the head of his opponent. Instead of music, blood flowed down the guitar.

After two days of rioting, Indira Gandhi was cremated amidst Vedic chants and hymns of the four religions. Sandalwood from the jungles of Mysore and roses from Kashmir Valley were flown in for the ceremony. Pure ghee churned from the milk of holy cows was poured on the pyre to kindle the flames. The sun was setting. The fire, swept by wind, leaped and crackled amidst slogans of *'Indira Gandhi amar rahay.'*

Heads of State flown in from all over the world watched the spectacle as if in an amphitheatre, the tragedy being performed on centre stage. Rajiv Gandhi circled the flaming pyre seven times with a calm face. The ritual confirmed Rajiv's inheritence. The mantle of power had fallen on his shoulders.

19

The monsoon rains were over. Delhi looked washed, the trees fresh and green. Orange tints of the mellowing sun shimmered in the air. The season of festivals had begun : dance dramas, Ramlila pageants, and the Diwali celebrations when even the poorest illuminates his house with clay lamps and merchants start new account books with a prayer to Lakshmi, the goddess of wealth.

There was a dinner at my house. The usual crowd of my friends: Uma Vasudev, the film theoretician Aruna who sat like a wise Mongolian cat holding a cigarette, princess Anita Singh, the famous dancers Indrani Rehman, Uma Sharma and Yamini Krishnamurti, a high government official, an art critic, a forester, a sociologist, an industrialist, and a few others.

We were busy in a heated discussion when I heard guffaws in my courtyard. I came out and met Satish Gujral and Kiran.

In the strong light of my verandah, Satish stared at Miro's Espana-82 poster in black, green and burning yellow. "Beautiful! What gaiety!" He chuckled, and sailed into the room.

He sat on the carpet, stretching out his legs. Leaning against my heavy steel almirah, he asked, "What have you stored in this steel locker? Money?"

"Yes, a lot of money." I teased him. In fact, I had stored blankets and quilts in it. He beamed, "So you are rich! I do not have a steel almirah like this, though I have built the Belgian Embassy."

We filled our glasses with whiskey, soda, beer, *nimboo paani*, and settled down.

"What's the latest?" Satish asked.

"The great news is that Ved Mehta has married a young American woman." said Uma.

Satish shook his head. "That's nothing! The greatest news is that in Bangladesh a one-hundred-and-fifteen-year-old mullah has married a girl of fourteen. His sons and grandsons attended the wedding."

Sakhish Pandit, well-dressed chief executive of a multinational company, laughed. "Then there is a chance for every one of us to marry six times. A man is never old."

"Lucky the girl who married Ved. He has waited for over forty years."

I had known Ved Mehta in New York and we—Uma, Aruna, the film actor Saeed Jaffri, his wife Madhur, the diplomat Natwar Singh—often attended parties at Ved's apartment. He talked proudly of his latest conquests, describing sexual details, how women would grab him at parties.

Uma leaned forward, "Have you read Ved's latest book?", She asked me.

"Why should I read Ved? Reading a second-rate writer is like being locked in conversation with a second-rate mind. It bores me."

"I think his writing is excellent. His books have won awards, special mention," said Aruna.

Satish burst out, "Nonsense! His writing has a false ring. He is blind, but he insists on describing the features of a man, the colour of his jacket, the cut of his beard. Hah! Simply a fraud!"

Aruna flicked her cigarette, "I think his writings are good!"

Satish's face twisted in disgust. "What writings? The West always lauds our second-rate talent, especially those who write against India. There has always been anti-India lobby in the white man's world. Indians were considered dirty, superstitious, uncultured bastards. They needed a Western polish. Previously there was Kipling ... Miss Mayo to champion the theory of the white man's burden. Then the West thought it best to beat India with its own stick. And who could be better for such a role than Indian writers? These writers fatten themselves on American money, sell well, and settle there. But in America they live an inferior life, always second-class citizens. They hate India, but have nothing else to sell except India. Who would read Ved Mehta if he were to write about New York?"

Indrani Rehman sipped her drink, catching up with the latest gossip and news. She had come from New York on one of her annual visits. Born of an American dancer mother and an Indian father, she had started learning dance at the age of five, married Habib Rehman, a dark Bengali Muslim architect, at sixteen, and was glittering on the Bharata Natyam stage by twenty-one. Tall, fair complexioned and supple-bodied, she had preserved her gorgeous form over the last three decades. She had brought her American disciple with her and was proudly displaying her at parties.

Speaking about her teaching methods, she said, "Our best tradition in the arts is the *guru-shishya parampara*. The disciple learns under the strict vigil of the guru—not in piecemeal lectures as in America—but by watching the guru, practising under him, listening to him, and grasping the art in total obedience and faith."

Uma Sharma, the Kathak dancer, cast a seductive glance, "Yes! this *parampara* is our glorious heritage. It has kept our art alive through *gharanas* ... the art passes from father to son, from the guru to his disciple. I'm a product of the great Lucknow *gharana*. I learned at the feet of guru Shambhu Maharaj."

Yamini Krishnamurti was sitting quiet as usual, listening to the glorification of dance *gharanas*. Suddenly her face changed into a scowl, "What guru and what *gharana* are you talking about? *Gharanas* create second-rate artists. It's always a great artist who creates a *gharana*. I have no *gharana*. I don't believe in this nonsense. I tell my disciples not to copy me. I teach them only grammar, and leave it to them to explore their own emotional and physic powers. Who can copy me? Only Yamini can copy Yamini. A *gharana* creates copies ... horrible carbon-copies. Our art world is full of such poor imitations!"

I was surprised by this dumb goddess who seldom opened her mouth at parties. Her viewpoint was offbeat, but true. Who was the *ustad* of Ghalib? Or Mir? Or Kalidasa? Or Tagore? Or Iqbal? No *gharanas,* no gurus.

The discussions rambled from dance to the statue of Mahatma Gandhi. Anita Singh, who had moved into her newly constructed marble-floored house and was decorating it with family heirlooms of paintings and sculptures said, "I think Gandhi's statue should be installed under the umbrella where once King George V stood in the royal robes facing India Gate. Gandhi should occupy the same seat of respect and be visible to millions during the Republic Day parade and Independence Day".

"That's absurd!" snapped Satish. "India Gate is not a site but a setting. If it were a site you could plant any statue there. But not in this setting. Gandhi will disturb the beauty of this architectural classic."

"Gandhiji deserves that place. After all, he is the father of the nation. Why should we grudge this place of honour to him? This is the best place to commemorate Gandhi."

"Anita, you have musical ears but visually you are blind. Let me talk to you in musical terms. If there is a grand composition of war music ... drums ... trumpets ... will you add a *Rama dhun* to it?"

The party roared with laughter. *Rama dhun* was Gandhiji's favourite tune, a sacred hymn he chanted while spinning.

The very idea of installing a Gandhi statue in front of the war memorial called India Gate was an affront to the apostle of Truth and Non-Violence. A contradiction ... Gandhi overseeing a Republic Day parade. Tanks going around his statue. Various architects of Delhi had voiced the same opinion. But politicians were set to place the statue of Gandhi under the royal canopy. Some suggested that the canopy be demolished and Gandhi sit cross-legged on the three-tiered platform. The politicians were divided. If Rajiv Gandhi said Gandhi's statue should be installed somewhere else, the Opposition roared with indignation, trying to catch the votes of the ignorant masses. Everything became an issue. Every incident, every event, every action, every calamity was converted into a vote-catching device. The Opposition condemned what Rajiv Gandhi did, and Rajiv condemned what the Opposition suggested. They were not opposite parties, but enemies. The national cause had no meaning for any one of them. It was a lust, a mania to rule the country. Corruption, horse-trading, bribes, and sex had moved in. The only object was to get votes and capture the throne.

I refilled my glass and turned around. Satish was locked in a violent argument with Man Mohan Singh, a cultural force in India's administrative service. He wrote poetry in English and was a keen bird-watcher. He wore a flamboyant turquoise turban, a plaid shirt, cravat, and a matching handkerchief in his breast pocket, He had been in Chandigarh when the Capital was being built.

"I disagree with you!" he fumed. "Chandigarh is beautiful, and we should be grateful to Corbusier. His concept of buildings on stilts, his symmetrical town planning and functional architecture—"

"Yes, yes!" Satish flared up. "We know all that! But he has saddled us with third-rate European architecture, which had already been rejected there. Just as the Americans dump frozen milk and wheat into the Third World which their pigs refuse to eat, so also Corbusier planted these box-type buildings in Chandigarh. He had tried to sell this design to Hitler, Stalin, Mussolini, and the French government. He went with his begging bowl even to Brazil. Finally it was Nehru who took the bait and bought his horrible architecture. An insult to our nation. A miserable, colourless and baseless architecture."

Indrani pushed back her jet-black hair and said, "I had dinner with Corbusier in 1950. He had come to India because he loved India and had a vision of creating a new city ... the City Beautiful. It was his dream. He believed in it. How can you say

that he wanted to con us?"
 Satish's mouth opened in a rage. "We are not judging the motives of Corbusier. An artist is not known for what he says but for what he creates. Dostoevsky was a gambler, spoke viciously against his friends, borrowed money right and left and never returned it, but was a great writer. Ghalib drank, made his house a gambling den and was jailed, but he was the greatest Urdu poet. I can give you countless examples of such artists. Genet was a pick-pocket, a homosexual, a man who loved treachery and betrayal, but a beautiful and great writer of plays. Sartre called him a saint ... I do not deny Corbusier's greatness. He was a master. A pioneer in many fields of architecture. But his Chandigarh is a disgrace. Architects are like actors. Every time Marlon Brando does a role he says, "This role has been my life's dream!" But sometimes he gives a poor performance. This does not mean that Brando is a poor actor. The same is true of Corbusier."
 "But —"
 "Don't interrupt me! Let me finish!" Satish waved his hand strongly, wiping out the protests of Indrani and the others. "Listen! Lutyens created the most beautiful Indo-British architecture, a classic of our times ... Rashtrapati Bhavan, the Secretariat, and Parliament House, with a mile-long vista of lawns and pools. He took care of the angles of mosques, mausoleums and ruins and integrated these in Delhi's body ...Lutyens hated India, but gave us a beautiful capital. Corbusier loved India, but gave us a third-rate Chandigarh!"
 Satish was speaking like a drunk. He glanced around and saw Man Mohan Singh's sullen face and wondered if he had offended this official who had purchased his three paintings for the Government of India's art galleries. Maybe tomorrow the government would decide to build a university ...or an art gallery

... or a museum ... or anything ... concerning architecture ...

Anita jumped into the fray. "I think Chandigarh is beautiful! It has fresh mountain air, spaces, lawns, avenues, Sukhna Lake, flowering trees ... I love the city."

"Have you seen Nek Chand's Rock Garden?" Satish asked. "See it ! It's a miracle. You know I am quite an egotist, but Nek Chand has made me feel so small. Nobody in India has a more original vision and greater genius than Nek Chand. His Garden is a fantasy. You cannot plan such a garden on paper. It has been designed stone by stone, shrub by shrub, pebble by pebble, stump by stump over the last forty years. Chandigarh is fortunate to have Nek Chand. Corbusier is shit!"

Man Mohan, Anita and Uma howled. Words flew like sparks in the smoke of the heated discussion. Satish glared at them. Blood rushed to his face. "I've sunk forty years of my life in design and architectural forms of which you know nothing. I am not talking in a gossip party. This is not a club. It's serious matter of art. My opinion is that of a professional. I cannot allow anybody to dominate and crush my views. I must speak!"

The art critic, who had three drinks, challenged, "You are talking only about multi-million dollar art. Who can afford to build palaces for a few rich people when millions are starving in huts? I believe in functional and democratic architecture."

Satish thundered, "Art is not democratic. Intellectuals like you have destroyed our architecture. For you architecture is a social science, making buildings to house the maximum number of people at the lowest cost. You see everything through a calculator. You have neither the eyes to see the beauty of the form, nor the mind to understand the design and visual aspects which determine sculpture, painting, architecture and graphic arts. But the intellectuals speak for hours at seminars without understanding. They cannot distinguish one pictorial form from the other. My bad work is praised and good rejected. Friends come to my house and pass through the hallway without looking at the walls. They gobble food, laugh, drink, crack jokes, and talk about art and politics. They come to the inauguration of an exhibition, drink coke, ogle, hug and backslap each other but do not go near the paintings. It's amazing how ignorant and pretentious our intellectuals are. They are the worst enemies of visual arts. They should be shot in a public square to silence their stupid tongues!"

The conversation turned to the recent killings of twenty-four bus passengers in Punjab which had rocked the throne in New Delhi. Rajiv Gandhi soothed the angry Members of Parliament by repeating, "Terrorism will be met severely! It will not be tolerated!" But people wanted action. Some miracle ... a solution. They organised peace marches, rallies, hunger strikes, and howled and clashed in the streets. The government blamed foreign powers. Pakistan, Canadian and American Sikhs. Terrorists. Killers. Misguided youths. These murders were treated as a *happening*, a phenomena of the contemporary world.

For the last ten years stray killings had been going on in Punjab. People were terror-stricken. A pall of gloom hung over the towns. People hurried home after sunset. Shopping centres were deserted ... thin traffic ... something ominous in the air ...

The Journalist said, "Why doesn't Rajiv Gandhi let the army loose in Punjab? We have a powerful army. Why can't it handle a few terrorists?"

The sociologist sucked at his pipe, "We cannot kill wantonly. We are a democracy. We cannot take the law in our hands and start the game of genocide. Let the violence come full circle."

"You want more violence? More bloodsehd? More murders? Bullshit! We have no guts. We read the Gita and preach non-violence. But the essence of the Gita is *action*. We have reversed its meaning. Gandhi was the culprit. He made the Gita a chant of *shanti* ... peace ... non-violence ..."

"If you don't have the guts to take a decision and act, you have no right to rule. In war, the commands are brief. You don't say, 'Please ... we'll be grateful if you would march forward.' You simply order: 'March!' 'Halt!' 'Attack!' We all know that the terrorists want Khalistan. A sovereign State. Nothing short of it. But your leaders scratch their balls for hours and make statements camouflaging reality. Don't bluff. Say it and do it!"

The forester, tall and wiry, with piercing eyes, said, "What's wrong with Khalistan? If Master Tara Singh had insisted on a Sikh State when the British were leaving, it would have been given to them on a platter. After all, the British had snatched Maharaja Ranjit Singh's Punjab by force and would be simply returning it to the rightful owners. Tara Singh was a sentimental fool. He believed in the promise of Mahatma Gandhi, a cunning lawyer-turned-politician, that the Sikhs would have a fair share in new India. What did they get? Insults. Humiliation. Jeers. Even brothers divide land. Why can't Sikhs have their share in this vast India?"

"You can't cut India into pieces. Can you chop off your hand? Or even a finger? India is one body."

"Nonsense! There is no such thing as one India. Unity in diversity ... many flowers blooming in the garden ... A bogus slogan! We are more alien to each other than people in Europe. Europe seems to me as one country. One culture. They have the same religion, same dress, same music and the same food habits. Emotionally, they are more united than us!"

"You cannot dismember a State. There will be chaos!"

"Read history! Empires have been breaking apart and coming together. New states are constantly being born. When

Pakistan was mooted in the thirties people laughed. 'How can you cut India into two,' they said. 'Hindus and Muslims are brothers. They have the same culture, same language, same music, same food habits. They have lived side by side for centuries, sharing each other's sorrows and happiness.' All that logic. All that sweet talk. Then the Muslims announced Direct Action. Knives flashed. Pandit Nehru and all the Congress leaders who had been denouncing the two-nation theory signed the pact. Pakistan was born overnight. Today, India seeks Pakistan's friendship. That's politics. I think the same situation is emerging in the case of Khalistan."

"There will *never* be a Khalistan!"

"Why not?"

"Impossible!"

"There *will* be a Khalistan! Nobody can stop it. Don't you see the writing on the wall? Read it. Already one-third of Punjab is under the influence of militants. They control it. Their writ runs. They order that girls will not wear jeans. The girls change their dress. Remove antennas and do not watch Doordarshan. People remove the antennas from their house tops. Militants hold court in villages and gurudwaras and pronounce judgements against which there is no appeal."

"Hindus are a nation of cowards!"

"What are you talking about? Nobody can be brave in front of a gun."

"Hindus are not empire builders. They have not conquered any country for the last two thousand years. Their minds are like cabbage. Always conquered by others. Right from Alexander the Great, to the Muslims and finally the British. The British swallowed the Maratha Empire, the Sikh Empire, the Mughal Empire and forged India into one. I think India will be better off if each linguistic state was independent. They will then think better, act better and love better."

"This crazy demand will let loose an orgy of killings!"

"You cannot establish a sovereign state without killing. I live in the forest. Do you know about trees and animals? Do you have any idea about their nature? We have killer trees who attack their progeny, suck their juices and become strong. Small trees pay homage to the king. So is the case with a tiger. When he sets up his sovereign territory, he marks it by urinating. Other animals sniff the urine and slink away. If another tiger dare enter the marked territory, the two fight a bloody war. The wolves, the elephants, the jackals, and birds do that. All use power to establish authority. The militants are doing the same."

"The world requires periodic blood-letting. Goddess Kali howls for blood. She can be appeased only by mass killings. The desire to kill is as strong in us as the desire to preserve. War is a necessity. Civilised nations, after years of peace, suddenly ache to kill. After a blood-bath, their passions subside. The cycle continues."

"Have you ever met a terrorist?" I said, "All revolutionaries are terrorists. They take up arms against the State. They are called killers. But if they win, they are honoured as patriots. A terrorist has a romantic halo because he fights for a cause.

"Damn it, what cause?"

"Well ... I always had a fascination for terrorists since my school days. Once I went to a pavement photographer who took pictures against a painted curtain. In those days the most popular pose of a terrorist was: a tipped hat, and a revolver in hand. I also got myself photographed in such a pose and sent it to the student leader Prabodh Chandra in Lahore, not realising that the revolver in my hand could have landed me in jail."

The forester said, "These militants are the hard core of

their community. You have to negotiate with them .. the fighting youth ... and not with Akali leaders who are above fifty—grey-bearded, paunchy, and nerveless. They let the rebel youth be butchered by the police without themselves shedding an ounce of blood. How can the youth allow these fogies to capture power?"

Aruna taunted me, "You are a Punjabi writer! Why don't you write about the killings in Punjab? It is a crime to keep mum when Punjab is burning."

"I know my people in Punjab," I said. If the problems are not tackled now, there will be a Khalistan. I had experienced exactly the same arguments, the same conversation, the same atmosphere in Lahore in the early forties. People scoffed at the idea of Pakistan. The Congress leaders called it treacherous and foolish. But then Radcliffe drew a line on the map, and in one stroke Pakistan was created. I tell you, Khalistan may become a reality in another fifteen years. And then there might be a demand from Muslims for Muqaddastan ... the land of the holy. It may sound idiotic ... Muslims may claim areas of their religious and historical glory. Ajmer Sharif, Nizamuddin Aulia, Red Fort, Jama Masjid, Taj Mahal, ... Fatehpur Sikri ... Meerut ... Moradabad ... Faizabad ... Imambaras of Lucknow ... Their heritage. Do you realise? Muslims feel that they have been crushed under the majority rule of Hindus for the past forty years. They are sixteen per cent of the population, but their voice in the government and military is hardly four per cent...After twenty years Muslims will swell to three hundred millions, five times that of France ... seven times of England ... thirty times that of Saudi Arabia ... and if they demand a separate State, we should not be shocked. Perhaps in twenty years there *will* be a Muqaddastan!"

Silence fell in the room.

20

I was shooting a TV serial when I received the news that my youngest brother Ram had died of a heart attack.

I cancelled everything and went to Bhatinda for the cremation. From my celluloid world, I came to the reality of dust and ashes. A fortnight of mourning.

Women came in groups from neighbouring villages and entered the street ululating, announcing their relationship in shrill wails. They wept as they hugged one another, sobbing, shuddering, beating their breasts.

The community *mirasan*, fat Muslim woman, her two front teeth missing, stood in the centre of the circle of mourners conducting the *siapa*. Virgins were not allowed to participate in this ritual. At the command of the *mirasan*, the women stripped off their shawls and blouses, their hair streaming down their huge naked breasts, and wailed collectively. Like an orchestra conductor, the *mirasan* led them in a symphony of wails, groans, shrieks, and gibbers. She gave orders in a fast rhythm and the women slapped their thighs, breasts, cheeks, and heads, and tore at their hair amidst wild howls.

After their grief subsided, they squatted on the floor, discussing Ram's last moments ... he was talking on the telephone making arrangements for his younger son's wedding when he felt a shooting pain in the chest and the telephone fell from his hand. He refused to be taken on a stretcher to the hospital and walked to the doctor. That proved fatal. Everything gone ... the wedding arrangements ... marigold ... the band he had arranged ... what can one do in the face of death?

An old woman sighed, "Ram had not seen the joys of life. But he died very peacefully. God is kind."

"The Brahmin was on time to trickle the holy water of the Ganges in Ram's mouth. Such souls go to heaven."

"When the wife of the grocer fell ill, she lingered on in bed for three months. An awful death. Must have committed sins in the previous life. God never pardons."

Then they started discussing their domestic problems, abductions, illness of their buffaloes, rains, daughters-in-law, and matrimonial proposals for their sons. Grief and the business of life went together.

Men sat separately in the adjoining room, making short comments with long pauses.

"Everyone has to go. But we fools do not know when."

"This sudden death is a blessing ... Only saints die like that ... a death without a sound or cry or pain."

"God should bless everyone with such an end!"

On the third day we went to the cremation ground to

collect Ram's ashes. A lanky black Brahmin splashed *Ganga jal* mixed with milk on the remains of my brother. Fumes and hissing sounds rose from the hot ashes. In the pale winter sun, women stood huddled in a corner with white shawls wrapped around their face.

The Brahmin—conductor of the funeral rites—raked the ashes with a wooden spade and started picking up the yellowed bones. My bald uncle joined in the sacred task. Seasoned in the ceremony of the dead, he picked a set of teeth. "These are Ram's teeth. Real? Or dentures?"

Fire had consumed the body; only the gleaming outline of his rib cage was intact. They picked up all the bones, down to the tiniest splinter, and put these in an iron pan. The Brahmin poured milky *Ganga jal* over them, rattled the bones between his palms, washed them three times, and started pounding them with a brass jug. The bones crackled and were reduced to tiny bits. He emptied the crushed bones into a red sheet and tied it with a black thread.

I took the bundle of bones, slung it on my shoulder and went straight to the railway station to catch the train to Haridwar to immerse the last remains of my brother in the waters of the Ganges.

All night I sat in the train dozing, holding the end of the twined sheet. The train swung, changing tracks, clanking and jolting. I had nightmarish images of fumes, fires, the black Brahmin, the dentures. The engine ran on like a drunken elephant, whistling and trumpeting as I sank deeper and deeper into depression ...

I reached Haridwar in the morning and saw the bluish-green hills and low ranges of the Himalays. A foggy red sun hung over them. Here the Ganges bursts out of the mountains and rushes foaming and tumbling down from the hills to become a half-mile-wide mass of water sweeping down the plains.

I was mobbed by a swarm of close-shaven, half-naked *pandas* (hereditary priests). Temple bells clanged, sadhus and women in white dhotis chanted hymns, and pilgrims in knee-deep water shouted *"Har har Gange, Har har Gange"*.

My family *panda* spotted me out in the crowd and quickly rattled off the names of my father, grandfather, great grandfather, village, caste, and subcaste. He held me by the arm and dragged me to his little stall shaded by a bamboo umbrella on the bank of the Ganges.

Pandas keep registers, a record of the family tree, on hand-made paper. This yellowed with age record treasures the names and signatures of the pilgrim's ancestors, their addresses, and dates of their visits to Haridwar, dating back to seven generations. Sometimes a *panda* sells his register to another *panda*. The new one takes over, preserving the records of families ... their roots ... their origins. These crumpled registers, brittle with age, clothbound in red, with two or three folds, open like a scroll—the account book of the dead.

I stood knee-deep in the sacred river, facing the sun, wearing a hand-spun khadi dhoti, a yellow chandan *tilak* on my forehead, and felt the cool waters lapping my naked legs. As the *panda* chanted Sanskrit *shlokas*, the waves swept away the ashes of my brother, some flowers, and a gold ring which he wore. It was considered holy that the dead carry a snippet of gold with them on their last journey.

After the rituals were over and the Brahmins fed, Ram's widow moved to Chandigarh to stay with her sons. The Bhatinda house—its courtyard, bedrooms, hallway, kitchen and sitting room—lay vacant. Sadness hovered over it, a musty oppressive smell which the dead leave behind.

My eldest brother Banarsi Das had died five years ago.

His widow had moved to stay with her daughter in Ludhiana. My third brother, Kewal, had left with his wife for California, where his son had settled as a doctor, leaving his ancestral roots for new moorings.

The three houses lay vacant. The wind moaned through them. The brothers had fought over the division of the joint family *haveli*, fought over each brick, each utensil, each wooden spoon, every inch of the joint land. Now this land was laying desolate. No one to own it.

When I returned to my courtyard I thought of my books, photos, precious slides and manuscripts. Awards and prizes. They will keep lying there till I am gone. Then the manuscripts and half-finished plays and awards will be flung into the dustbin.

It was evening. I sat in the wicker chair in my courtyard. My mind was in a haze ... Everything was changing ... I saw my face in the mirror while shaving. It was the face of an alien ... a different man ... the beautiful Parveen Babi had become enormously fat ... her glossy hair ratty and snarled, her face ballooned, abnormal. The DOUBLE had taken over. Everything had changed. Communism had committed hara-kiri in Russia. Lenin's tall statue pulled down by a noose around his neck ... Impossible ... Impossible .... Thirty years ago in a heated discussion with writers in this very room I had laughed at the word 'impossible'. Everything was possible. Life was moving ... changing tracks ... heading towards a blind alley.

The skyline was flushed. Shadows deepened and the moon arose in the sky, its edges smudged. Moon-beams hit the red stone slabs of a newly-constructed skyscraper and reflected a purple light into my courtyard ... purple smoke rising ... images of the past glimpsed ... people and events, passions, frustrations ... all governed by accidents over which I had no control... The past flowed through me ... dream images I carried in my head. I wanted to sacrifice my life for a dream, which might have been a stone, an idea, a revolution, a flag or a woman. Tagore's lines "Oh woman, you are half woman and half dream,' rang in my head. I was searching for an altar, to lay down my life at the feet of a beautiful woman whom I had invested with glamour in my imagination.

Twenty years later I met Barbara and was aghast ... a white-haired, snaggle-toothed witch, hobbling in my courtyard ... twenty years ago in this very courtyard I had made love to her, and thought of her as a most sexy female. Now she looked hideous, specially her toothy smile. How could I have loved this woman? Her conversations, repeating the same phrases, were disgusting. How could I have wasted my life on this creepy female?

I tracked back the images of my life ... a long film strip running backward ... watching these lived-in images was soothing ... Krapp's Last Tape ... I plunged into the beauty of these days ... images I wanted to relive ... even that snaggle-toothed female ... those sensations, tortures ... the tearing of flesh, its bliss. In the arms of that woman when she was youthful and walked with a swing ... walking with me on the Konark beach, naked in the wind-swept night ... her hair flying ... she laughed and stripped me ... I felt suddenly liberated ...the salty cool air slapped my body ... her wicked intelligence and inborn cunning tempting me.

If God had told me that this life was a rough sketch, and granted me another, would have I avoided the pitfalls and mistakes I had committed? *Never!* I would not barter it for any other life. I would want to live exactly the same life I had lived. I would like to squander my money, my time, my **being**, and taste the same tortures and bliss rooted in my flesh ... again fall in love with the same woman I had met at a picnic party ... we flew to Kashmir ... house boat ... moonlight ... passion ... the following evening she became my enemy, full of jealousy and hate ... then she wept and begged my pardon ... Again my courtyard ... making love with all her fury ... jasmine buds and their swooning sweet fragrance ... she loved to rub jasmine on her nipples, the smell evoking memories ...

Living in those memories ... under the grip of this woman for years ... She betrayed me and spent my money and left me for a fat Gujarati film maker who promised her stardom ... she walked like a docile mare into his stable ... I was lusting for her, consumed by jealousy, constantly thinking of her ... living those moments again and again in an unending cycle ... a blind passion ... one night of love making with her was worth thirty years of life ... its burning bliss still throbbing in my veins ... breathing through layers of other experiences ... the taste of her mouth ... fragrance of her body ... her hair ... her lips ... they never died.

Suddenly I thought of my death. What would I be thinking on my death bed? What sensations ... what images ... perhaps this woman will appear before my dying eyes ... her face slowly fading into eternity ... the last glimpse ... the last reality ... also the snaggle-toothed Barbara ... and that actress for whom I played Pygmalion ... a blur of faces ... my son's youthful face smiling ... his dimpled chin and sensuous smile ... he had some of my own features refined and brightened and made more beautiful by a mix of billions of cells ... my own rebirth ...

INDEX

Abbas, Khwaja Ahmed, 30, 78
Actor Prepares, An, 33
Acropolis, 99
Africa, 57
Ajmer Sharif, 177
Ajmeri Gate, 154, 155
Akal Takht, 159
Akhtar, Begum, 26, 134
Alexanderovna, Effonina, 29, 30, 32, 33
Alkazi, E, 115, 120
All India Radio, 17, 18, 157
America, 79, 166
America, America, 95, 96, 97, 98
American Embassy, 91
American Sikhs, 173
American visit, 87, 88, 89
Amritsar, 19, 67
Anand, Mulk Raj, 2, 3, 4, 5, 6, 7, 8, 21, 47, 78
Andes, 25
Aragon, Louis, 25
Ataturk, Kemal, 17
Athens, 97, 98, 99
Aza, 34
Azerbaijanis, 33

Babi, Parveen, 137, 138, 139, 140, 142, 145, 182
Baliga, Dotor, 28
Blau, Herbert, 54
Bangladesh, 165
Bangladesh war, 118
Barbara, 183, 184
Barkan, 34, 35
Basil, Saint, 31, 36, 38
Beckett, 55
Bedi, Rajinder Singh, 6, 17, 18
Belgian Embassy, 148
Bentley, Eric, 50, 53
Berens, Ralph, 91, 92, 93
Berlin, 49, 51, 52, 59
Berlin Youth Festival, 9

Bhagat, Usha, 116, 117, 118, 120, 131
Bhan, Suraj, 115
Bharata Natyam, 7, 167
Bhatia, Sheila, 131
Bhatinda, 77, 178, 181
Bhawalpur, 132
Bikaner, 132
Black Shalwar, The, 154
Bombay, 2, 3, 5, 17, 18, 25, 28, 72, 73, 74, 75, 77, 137, 138, 139
Brando, Marlon, 171
Brazil, 170
Brecht, 52, 54, 67
BBC, 158,
Brook, Peter, 5
British Museum, 98, 99
Buddha, 17
Budenny, Marshal 13
Bukharin, 7
Butalia, Subhadra, 158

Calcutta, 66
California, 182
Cat on a Hot Tin Roof, 96, 97
Caucasian Chalk Circle, The , 54, 59
Chandigarh, 117, 118, 125, 126, 170, 181
Chandra, Prabodh, 176
Chaplin, Charlie, 49
Chatterjee, Sarat Chandra, 93
Chattopadhyaya, Kamla Devi, 121
Chekhov, Anton, 29, 30, 93
Chenab river, 34
China, 61
Chinese calligraphy, 59
Chinese Writers Union, 58
Chopra, 128
Churchill's prophecy, 143
Communist Party, 88
Communist Party of India, 18
Congress Party, 22
Connaught Lane, 163
Connaught Place, 2, 11

INDEX

Corbusier, 170, 171
Cottage Emporium, 80
Cremation ground, Delhi, 110, 111
Cultural Revolution, 59
Czar, 30
Czarist rule, 31

Danjuro, 107
Danube, 63
Das, Banarsi, 181
de Silva, Anil, 3
Dehlvi, Sadia, 153
Delhi, 1, 2, 4, 10, 19, 20, 28, 34, 35, 62, 71, 74, 75, 110, 114, 115, 126, 154, 159, 165, 173
Delia del Carril, 62
Department of Indian Theatre, 113
Desai, Morarji, 122
Dhawan, R.K. 122
Diwali, 73, 165
Don Juan in Russian Style, 37
Doris, 57
Dostoevsky, 171

Ehrenburg, Ilya, 6, 7, 8
Eisenstein, 121
El Cubano, 55
Elgin, Lord, 98
Emergency, 112, 122
Emi, Siao, 59
England, 11
Europe, 5, 46, 156, 174

Faiz, 26
Faizabad, 177
Fatehpur Sikri, 177
Films Division, 148
Film Festival Directorate, 109
Fine Arts Theatre, 68
Florence, Miss, 11

Florida, 94
Frederichstrasse, 50

G B Road, 154
Gandhi, Indira, 112, 114, 115, 117, 119, 121, 123, 128
  cremation of, 163, 164
  murder of, 158, 159, 160
Gandhi, Mahatma, 2, 11, 12
  fast unto death by, 13
Gandhi movement, 13
Gandhi's song, 13
Gandhi statue
  discussion on, 168, 169, 170
Gandhi, Rajiv, 163, 164, 169, 170, 173, 174
Ganga Jal, 180
Garga, Bhagwan, 54
Gargi, Balwant, 5, 21, 56, 88, 91, 95, 105, 113, 114, 116, 128, 133, 137, 160, 161
Genet, 55, 170
George, 87
George, King V, 169
Ghalib, 94, 168, 171
Giraudoux's *Tiger at the Gates*, 58
Gita, The, 174
Glider, Miss Ross, 94, 95
Gogh, Van, 16
Gogol, 29, 42
Golden Notebook, The, 55
Golden Temple, 159
Gopal, Dr S, 144
Gorakhpuri, Firaq, 78
Gorky, 29
Grass is Singing, 57
Great Dictator, The 49
Great Wall of China, 59
Greece, 99
Greenwich Village, 92
Grewal, Mohanjeet, 141, 142
Guillen, Nicholas, 47, 48

INDEX

Gujral, Satish, 74, 75, 90, 146, 148, 149, 150, 166, 167, 170, 171, 172
Gujrat, 34
Gupta, Urmila, 109
Gupta, Tara Chand, 11
Gypsy Theatre, Moscow, 33, 35, 44, 89

Haider, Niaz, 67
Hall, Peter, 57
Handoo, H K, 10
Hapgood, Elizabeth, 33
Haridwar, 180, 181
Hazrat Chishti, 131
Hamburg, 157
Hermeline, Steffan, 47
Hiroshima, 106
Hitler, 12, 170
Hotel Ukrainiya, 35
Hungarian upsurge, 89, 90
Hurwicz, Angelica, 49, 53, 54
Hyde Park, 56

Ibsen, 29
Imroz, 71, 72, 74, 75, 76, 77, 78, 79
Independence Day, 169
India Gate, 31, 169
India International Centre, 158
India Today, 149
Indian Embassy, 44
India's kathak dancers, 60
International Peace Conference, 77
Iqbal, 16, 17, 93, 94, 168
Islam, 17
Islamabad, 154

Jafri, Ali Sardar, 6, 8, 15, 26, 30, 78
Jaffri, Saeed, 166
Jalandhar, 134, 135
Jamia Milia, 67

Jamaluddin, 154
Janta wave, 122
Jannat, 126
Japan, 106, 121
Jeannie, 114, 117, 118, 119
Jesus, 115
Jhabwala, Ruth, 93
Joan, 57
John, 141, 144, 145
Juliot-Curie, 25

Kabir, 94
Kabuki, 53, 106, 107
Kalidasa, 67, 94, 168
Kamani, 35
Kamil, Tara Singh, 81, 82
Kapurthala, 154
Karle caves, 5, 6
Kashmir, 184
Kashmiri, Agha Hashr, 67
Kaval, Khushwant's wife, 144, 145, 153, 157
Kazan, Elia, 94, 96, 98, 100, 109, 110, 111, 112
Kennedy, John F, 140
Kewal, 182
Khalistan, 174, 176
Khan, Genghis, 63
Khan, Sanjay, 1, 37
Khandala, 5
Khruschev, 89
  visit to India, 18
Kipling, 167
Kiran Gujral, 148 149, 166
Korean war, 89
Kremlin, 30, 31, 36, 41
Krishan Chander, 6
Krishnamurti, Yamini, 165, 168
Kusum, 131

Lahore, 1, 3, 11, 13,
Lal, Bansi, 117

INDEX

Lal, Kishori, 101, 102
Lal Chand, 12
Lalu Ram, 67
Lan-feng, Mei, 60
Leicester Square, 55
Lenin's tomb, 31
Lessing, Doris, 55, 56
Life magazine, 141
Lincoln Centre, 56
Litto, 9, 10
Loden, Barbara, 110
London, 3, 44, 54, 55, 56, 58, 98, 144, 176, 177
London Theatre, 57
Lorca, Garcia, 25
Ludhiana, 134, 135, 182
Lumumba, Patrice, 77, 78
Lutyen, 171

Macbeth, film on, 58
Macchu Picchu, ruins of, 25
McDonald, 92
Madhya Pradesh, 67
Maharaj, Shambhu, 168
Mangala, 101, 102
Mangeshkar, Lata, 134
Mangolian population, 63
Manhattan, 99
Mann, Paul, 95, 96
Manto, Saadat Hasan, 93, 94, 154
Manu, 1, 26
Mao, 59
Mao's Red Book, 16
Maratha Empire, 175
Marg office, 3
Maupassant, 33, 93, 104
Mausoleum of Lenin, 30
Mausoleum of Stalin, 30
Mayo, Miss, 167
Meerut, 177
Mehta, Ved, 93, 166, 167
Mexico, 121
Mir, 168

Mirza Sahiban, 122
Mishima, Yukio, 105, 106, 107
Mitti ki Gaadi, 67, 68
Modigliani, 144
Moradabad, 177
Moraes, Frank, 7
Moscow Art Theatre, 33, 41
Moscow, purges in 1936, 7
Moscow Theatres, 153
Moscow visit, 28, 35, 89
Moscow women, 47
Moskva Airport, 41
Mother Courage, 50, 52
Mughal architecture, 97
Mughal empire, 175
Miller, Arthur, 110
Mussolini, 170

Naipaul, 93
Nanak, Guru, 17
Nanda, Gulzari Lal, 84
Narayan, R K, 93
Nargis, 143
Natasha, 32, 33
Nehru, Jawaharlal, 10, 25, 28, 68, 170, 175
  death of, 80, 81, 85
Nehru's government, 11
Nek Chand's Rock Garden, 172
Neruda, Pablo, 24, 27, 25, 47, 48, 61, 62, 87
New York, 91, 94, 98, 99, 105, 110, 141, 167,
New York publishers, 87, 89, 91
Newsweek, 149
Nimmo, 155
Nizamuddin Aulia, 177
Noonan, Tom, Cultural Counsellor, 90

Observer, The, 57
Oh Calcutta, 58
Olga Knipper-Chekhova, 30
Orozco, 150

INDEX

Osborne, 55
Ostrovsky, 29
Oxford Street, 55

Pacific Ocean, 63
Paintings on partition, 90
Pakistan, 2, 132, 154, 173, 175
Parikshat, Prince, 159
Pandit, Sakhish, 131, 166
Paris, 24, 118, 141, 150
Paris Match, 31
Parliament House, 144, 171
Patiala, 10, 159
Paul, 97, 98
Peace Dove, 26, 33
Peace movement, 8, 90
Peace rally, 98, 90
Peking, 58, 59, 62
Perin, 9
Peshawar, 133
Peter Hall, 55
Petrograd, 29
Petrova, Olga, 34
Picasso, 26, 144
Picasso's art, 33
Picasso Dove, 25, 49
Piccadilly, 55
Poland, 47
Polish women, 47
Press censorship, 112
Prime Minister's House, 118
Prison life, 11, 12, 13
Pritam, Amrita, 70, 71, 72, 73, 74, 76, 78, 79
Prostitute and the Yogi, The, 157
Prostitution, 155, 156, 157
Panjab University, 113, 125
Punjab, 66, 133
Punjab killings, 173, 174, 175, 176

Queensway (now Janpath) 2

Radcliffe, 177
Radhakrishnan, Dr 144
Rahul, 120
Ralph, 95
Ram, 178, 179, 180, 181
Ram Lila grounds, 78
Rashtrapati Bhavan, 171
Ray, Satyajit, 97, 121, 149
Red Fort, 177
Red Square, 31, 32
Red Star, 31, 36
Redgrave, Michael, 58
Rehman, Habib, 167
Rehman, Indrani, 121, 165, 170, 171
Renuka, 155
Reshma, 130, 131, 133, 134
Rhodesia, 56
Riots, 159, 160, 163
  see Gandhi, Mrs
Robert McGregor and George, 87
Rodkar, Joan, 55
Russia, 7, 63, 64, 88
  harakiri in, 182

Sahir, 26, 78
Sahitya Akademy Board, 88
Sakshi, 21, 22, 4, 46, 47, 48
Salem jail, 16
Santiniketan, 123
Sayers, Tana, 57
Sea Gull, The , 29
Seaton, Marie, 120
Seattle, 126
Seghers, Anna, 47
Schmitz, kittty, 49, 50
Shah Commission, 122
Shakespeare, 29
Sham Lal, 80
Shama, Urdu magazine, 71
Shanghai, 59
Shankar, Ravi, 16
Sharma, Uma, 165, 168

Shaw, 29, 67
Shudraka, 67
Siberia, 31
Sikh Empire, 165
Sikhs killings, 159, 160, 161
Singh, Anita, 154, 155, 165, 168, 172
Singh, Giani Zail, 117
Singh, Gulzar, 81, 82, 85, 104, 162, 163
Singh, Gurcharan, 73
Singh, Inderjit, 12
Singh, Joginder, 12, 13, 14, 15
Singh, Khushwant, 80, 81, 139, 140, 142, 143, 153, 156
Singh, Krishanjit, 81, 82
Sindhu, Madan Bala, 131
Singh, Maghar, 127, 158, 160
Singh, Maharaja Ranjit, 174
Singh, Man Mohan, 170, 171
Singh, Master Tara, 174
Singh, Mubarak, 19, 20, 21
Singh, Navtej, 12, 14, 26
Singh, Natwar, 166
Singh, Raja Padamjit, 154
Singh, Tara, 160, 161, 162
Smirnoff, 44
Sohini Mahiwal, 34
Soviet Land, The, 89
Soviet Marshal, 13
Soviet Writers' Union, 89
Stalin, 8, 13, 17, 31, 141, 170
Stanislavsky, 34
Stork, 88, 91
Street Car Named Desire, A, 96
Sultan Razia play, 115, 120
Svetlana, 35, 36
Sweden
  no prostitution in, 156

Tagore, Rabindranath, 90, 123, 124, 168
Taj Hotel, 4, 128
Taj Mahal, 177
Tandon, 127
Tarvir, Habib, 35, 36, 37, 66, 67, 121

Teheran, 44
Thapar, Raj, 6
Thapar, Romesh, 6
Tiger at the Gates, 58
Time, 149
Tiwari, Vishwanath, 143
Tolstoy, 29
Tottenham Court Road, 54
Toulouse-Lautrec, 144, 150
Turgenev, 29
Tynan, Kenneth, 55, 57, 58
Tzu' hsi, 60

Ulan Bator, 62
Urrutia, Matilde, 62

Vajfdar, Roshan, 6
Van-Gogh, 149
Vasudev, Aruna, 165, 166, 177
Vasudev, Uma, 131, 152, 155, 165, 166, 167
Verma, 128
Vimla, 9
Vogue, magazine, 33

Waiting for Godot, 57
Warsaw Youth Festival, 46
Weigel, Helene, 53
Williams, Tennessee, 94, 96, 97
World Peace Council 24
World War, 59, 64

Yamuna bridge, 160, 162
Yangtze River, 59

Zaheer, Sajjad, 78
Zaidi, Begum Qudsia, 67, 68
Zen Painter Chi Pai-Shea, 60
Zia Saheb, 132, 135